MODERN DAY
Quilter

Modern Day Quilter

Landauer Publishing, www.landauerpub.com, is an imprint of Fox Chapel Publishing Company, Inc.

Project Team
Managing Editor: Gretchen Bacon
Acquistions Editor: Amelia Johanson
Editor: Christa Oestreich
Designer: Freire Disseny + Comunicació
Indexer: Jay Kreider

ISBN 978-1-63981-033-8

Library of Congress Control Number: 2023944257

We are always looking for talented authors. To submit an idea, please send a brief inquiry to acquisitions@foxchapelpublishing.com.

Note to Professional Copy Services:
The publisher grants you permission to make up to six copies of any quilt patterns in this book for any customer who purchased this book and states the copies are for personal use.

Printed in China
First printing

MODERN DAY
Quilter

16 Patchwork Quilts and
Projects for Everyday Life

KILEY FERONS

Contents

Welcome to My Modern-Day Quilting

What makes a quilt or quilter "modern"? The definition of modern is "up to date, current, trending, or involving recent techniques, methods, or ideas." Quilting has been around for a very long time. I'd even venture to say that there aren't very many (if any) brand-new ideas or techniques for quilting, just new ideas on how to use those techniques.

In this book, you will find sections of various quilting techniques. I will introduce each technique and give instructions on how to accomplish them. Then, I will follow with a modern quilt or quilted project to help you practice these techniques. Some projects are quick and easy, and some will take time. But none are too difficult for any novice to try.

Over time we see trends come and go. But you'll probably also notice that trends have a habit of coming back around eventually. Puff quilts were popular 20–30 years ago. It wasn't until recently that they have been making a reappearance as a "modern" trend. What makes them modern if it is an old technique? It's all about your vision and how you execute it. A modern puff quilt uses modern fabrics, ombres, or trendy colors, and we all "ooh and ahh" over how cute and modern it is!

During the pandemic, the quilting community saw a huge upswing in new quilters. I love to see so many people finding joy and creativity through this medium. And, as a modern-day quilter, I want to share the techniques I have come to learn and love, but with a modern spin.

The point of this book is to show modern quilters how having an arsenal of skills in your back pocket can broaden your horizons and open doors to so much more creativity and joy. Even though many of these techniques are as old as time, it is the vision and execution that make them modern.

I can't wait to see your vision and execution of these fun quilts and projects! Be sure to share them with me by tagging me on social media at @kileysquiltroom.

—Kiley Ferons

My Favorite Tools

Having the right kind of tools makes all the difference when quilting. I have used many brands and tools over the years and have settled on some of my favorites that I just can't bear to live without!

- **Creative Grids® rulers** are my favorite brand, as they have a textured back to keep the ruler from slipping. Their Stripology® Ruler is fantastic. It makes quick work of cutting up your strips and subcutting them.

- **Rotary cutters** are a *must*. Someone recently asked me where I got my "fabric pizza cutter," and that's just about the best thing anyone has ever asked me! So go get yourself a good sharp "fabric pizza cutter."

- **Large cutting mat.** I don't particularly care for any one brand of cutting mat. The more important thing is to have a big one. The bigger the mat, the fewer times you'll need to fold a piece of fabric to cut it. I use a 36" mat.

- **Iron.** Any iron with fabric settings will do. I don't use steam settings. Instead, I just use a spray or misting bottle of water.

- **Ironing surface.** I have a large side table that I converted into an ironing surface with fabric storage (which you can read about on my blog), but a regular ironing board will do just fine. You can also use a wool pressing mat.

- **Thread.** I like to piece with a neutral color (like cream or gray) so it won't stand out too obviously if a seam shows on the front. You may also consider a darker thread if most of your fabrics in your quilt are darker, or a white if most of your fabrics are fairly light. When quilting, I try to pick something that matches the fabric better.

- **Batting.** I love a nice, soft, malleable batting. Hobbs Heirloom® Premium 100% Cotton is my favorite. But anything that is at least 80% cotton will do.

- **Fabric.** Obviously, this is important to be able to make any of these projects! You can use any "quilting cottons" that are a higher thread count than the general cottons you'll find in the craft section at your local department store.

- Last, but not least, you need a **seam ripper**. I love the seam rippers with a rubber bulb on them that help you gather up all your threads when you're done with your "booboo." But my favorite seam ripper is a gorgeous handmade-wood one from Modern American Vintage. It came in a set with a point turner and hera marker. I love it because it's beautiful and has a larger handle on it, which makes it easier to grip.

These are all the basic necessities. As you go through this book, you'll find a few projects here and there that require some other materials. Make sure you read the project materials lists before embarking on your next project!

This Stripology ruler is perfect for cutting strips because it buffers a rotary cutter on either side, keeping the lines straight.

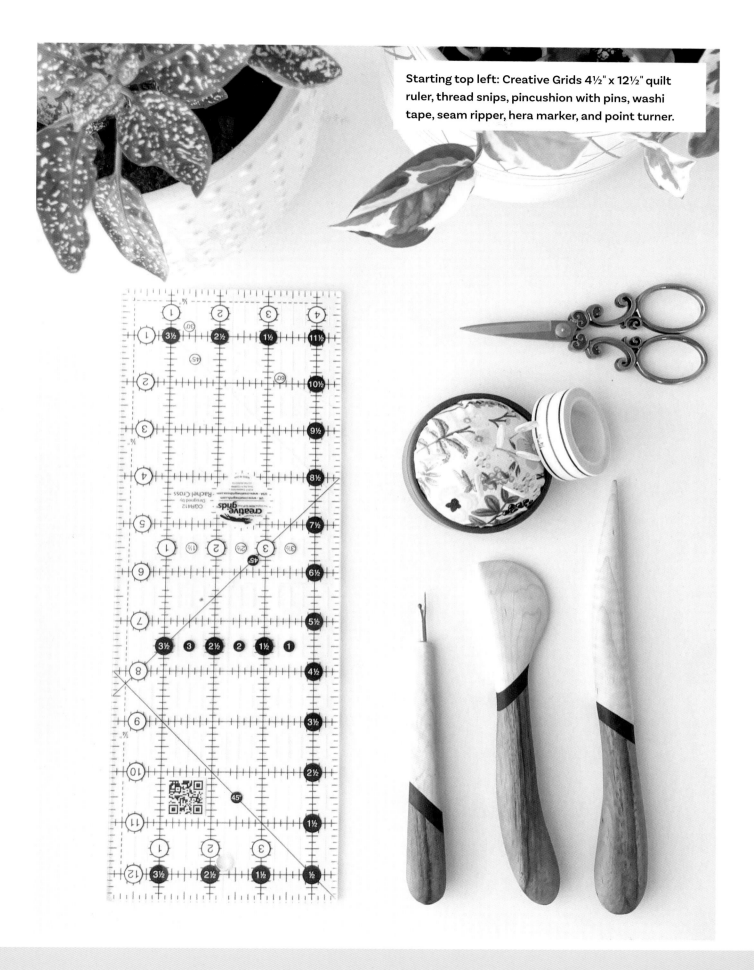

Starting top left: Creative Grids 4½" x 12½" quilt ruler, thread snips, pincushion with pins, washi tape, seam ripper, hera marker, and point turner.

Intro to HSTs

Mastering the **Half-Square Triangle (HST)** is an essential and foundational skill to have as a quilter. It is one of the most basic blocks, which can be used to create any number of designs and patterns depending on how you arrange them. You can try making a bunch of HSTs yourself and arrange them however you want and see what kind of designs you can come up with!

There are several different ways to create HSTs. Below you will find several methods for creating HSTs. Making multiple HSTs at once will help you save time, but you can decide which methods you prefer!

One at a Time

You can create HSTs from any two same-sized squares. Place them together with Right Sides Together (RST). Mark a diagonal line and then sew on the diagonal. Trim off the excess as shown. Press the seam to one side.

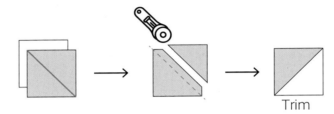

Trim

Two at a Time

Place two same-sized squares together, RST. Mark a diagonal line on the back of the lighter fabric, and sew ¼" away from the line on both sides. Cut on the line. Open your HSTs and press the seams to one side. Trim off the excess. Trim HSTs to indicated size.

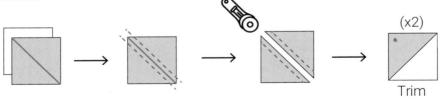

(x2)

Trim

Four at a Time

Place two same-sized squares together, RST. Mark two diagonal lines through the center. Sew ¼" away from all four sides. Cut on each of the diagonal lines you drew. Open your HSTs and press the seams to one side. Trim excess from the seam. Trim HSTs to indicated size.

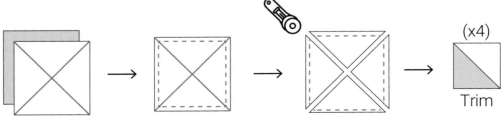

(x4)

Trim

Eight at a Time

Place two same-sized squares together, RST. Mark two diagonal lines and two perpendicular lines through the center. Sew ¼" away from both sides of each diagonal line (diagonal lines only). Cut on each of the lines you drew. Open your HSTs and press the seams to one side. Trim off the excess. Trim HSTs to indicated size.

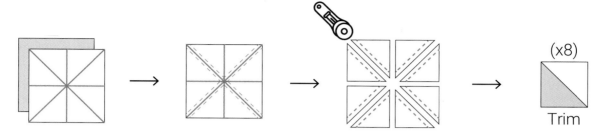

Trim

Always make sure to trim your HSTs before using them in a quilt to ensure accuracy and to reduce bulk in your seams.

Even though the HST is such a traditional and quintessential block, it can be used as a foundation to create many modern works of art! Let's dive into some quilts and projects that use HSTs.

Countdown Chain

My kids love to make paper chains for all kinds of occasions: birthdays, holidays, vacations, or even when Grandma and Grandpa are coming to visit! These countdown chains are a perfect reusable option for helping kids visualize the passing of time in a fun way! We use the one-at-a-time HST method (page 10) in this project.

Before You Start

Read through all the directions and steps before you start. All seams are sewn with a ¼" seam allowance. **All templates need to be printed at 100%** and *not* "fit to page." You can adjust this in your printer settings. Verify that your template is printed at the correct size by measuring all sides of the 1" reference square.

To make 30 chain links, you'll need 30 assorted fabric scraps. You can use scraps, coordinating fabrics, or even all one fabric.

For more inspiration, check out the hashtag #countdownchain and #kileysquiltroom. Be sure to use these when you post pictures of your quilt to share with others!

WOF = Width of Fabric
RST = Right Sides Together

Supplies

Template (page 110)

¾ yard colored fabric or scraps, subcut:
- (60) 2½" x 2½"
- (60) 2½" x 3½"
- (30) 2½" x 10½"
- Each chain link will use (2) 2½" x 2½", (2) 2½" x 3½", and (1) 2½" x 10½" pieces, so plan your scraps accordingly if you want them to match.

⅓ yard white or white scraps, subcut:
- (30) 2½" x 4½"

(30) 1" squares of Velcro®, cut from a roll

Permanent fabric pen or marker

Making the Chains

1. Mark a diagonal line on the back of all colored 2½" x 2½" squares. Place one on the left side of each 2½" x 4½" white rectangle. Sew on the diagonal line. Press the seam to the dark side and trim excess, leaving a ¼" seam allowance. Do the same on the other end of the white rectangle, making sure that the diagonal lines are going the same direction.

2. Sew a 2½" x 3½" colored rectangle to each side of the previous unit. Press seams.

3. Place each constructed piece RST with a colored 2½" x 10½" rectangle. Use the *Countdown Chain Template* to round the corners. Then sew a ¼" seam allowance all the way around the two pieces, leaving a 1½" gap on one side.

4. Flip the entire construction right side out and press. Fold in the gap edges and top stitch right along the edge, all the way around the chain.

5. Sew one side of a Velcro square to each end of the chain, one on the front and one on the back. Sew the Velcro around all the edges. For extra security, you can sew an X through the square as well. Be sure to use coordinating thread so it blends into the fabric.

6. Use a permanent fabric pen or marker to write the numbers on the white spaces of your chains. You can go in color order, mix them up, or make it however you want it to look when they are all chained together!

Pothos Quilt

Indoor gardening and quilting are my two main hobbies. When given the chance, I love to bridge the gap! This quilt is inspired by a common and well-loved indoor plant called a pothos. They are great for bookshelves or hanging pots because they extend their vines down so beautifully.

As you can see, this pattern was designed to look like the vines of a pothos plant. It is made up entirely of half-square triangles; therefore, this is a great practice exercise on perfecting them!

Before You Start

Read through all the directions and steps before you start. All seams are sewn with a ¼" seam allowance.

For more inspiration, check out the hashtag #pothosquilt and #kileysquiltroom. Be sure to use these when you post pictures of your quilt to share with others!

WOF = Width of Fabric
RST = Right Sides Together
HST = Half-Square Triangle

FABRIC REQUIREMENTS

	Throw 52" x 56"	Twin 65" x 87"	Queen 91" x 96"
Dark Color	½ yard	½ yard	¾ yard
Medium Color	¾ yard	¾ yard	1¼ yards
Light Color	½ yard	½ yard	¾ yard
Background	3¼ yards	5¼ yards	6¼ yards
Backing	3½ yards	6 yards	8¼ yards
Binding	½ yard	⅔ yard	¾ yard

CUTTING INSTRUCTIONS

	Throw 52" x 56"	Twin 65" x 87"	Queen 91" x 96"
Dark Color	(2) 6" x WOF, subcut: (12) 6" x 6"	(2) 7" x WOF, subcut: (12) 7" x 7"	(3) 9" x WOF, subcut: (12) 9" x 9"
Medium Color	(3) 6" x WOF, subcut: (16) 6" x 6"	(3) 7" x WOF, subcut: (16) 7" x 7"	(4) 9" x WOF, subcut: (16) 9" x 9"
Light Color	(2) 6" x WOF, subcut: (8) 6" x 6"	(2) 7" x WOF, subcut: (8) 7" x 7"	(2) 9" x WOF, subcut: (8) 9" x 9"

Background

(6) 6" x WOF, subcut:
(37) 6" x 6"
(18) 2½" x WOF, subcut:
(2) 2½" x 42½" **A**
(2) 2½" x 16½" **B**
(11) 2½" x 14½" **C**
(5) 2½" x 12½" **D**
(3) 2½" x 10½" **E**
(3) 2½" x 8½" **F**
(30) 2½" x 4½" **G**
(51) 2½" x 2½" **H**
(2) 10½" x WOF,
sew strips end to end
and subcut:
(1) 10½" x 48½" **J**
(1) 4½" x 4½" **K**
(1) 4½" x 6½" **L**
(1) 4½" x 10½" **M**

(7) 7" x WOF, subcut:
(37) 7" x 7"
(4) 3" x WOF,
sew strips end to end
and subcut:
(2) 3" x 70" **A**
(16) 3" x WOF, subcut:
(2) 3" x 20½" **B**
(11) 3" x 18½" **C**
(5) 3" x 15½" **D**
(3) 3" x 13" **E**
(3) 3" x 10½" **F**
(30) 3" x 5½" **G**
(51) 3" x 3" **H**
(2) 30" x WOF,
sew strips end to end
and subcut:
(1) 30" x 60½" **J**
(1) 5½" x 5½" **K**
(1) 5½" x 8" **L**
(1) 5½" x 13" **M**

(6) 9" x WOF, subcut:
(37) 9" x 9"
(4) 4" x WOF,
sew strips end to end
and subcut:
(2) 4" x 72" **A**
(24) 4" x WOF, subcut:
(2) 4" x 28½" **B**
(11) 4" x 25½" **C**
(5) 4" x 21½" **D**
(3) 4" x 18" **E**
(3) 4" x 14½" **F**
(30) 4" x 7½" **G**
(51) 4" x 4" **H**
(3) 16" x WOF,
sew strips end to end
and subcut:
(1) 16" x 84½" **J**
(1) 7½" x 7½" **K**
(1) 7½" x 11" **L**
(1) 7½" x 18" **M**

Half-Square Triangles

You need:

- 95 Dark-Colored HSTs (there is 1 leftover)

- 128 Medium-Colored HSTs

- 63 Light-Colored HSTs (there is 1 leftover)

Place each 6" x 6" colored square RST with a 6" x 6" background square. Use the eight-at-a-time HST method (page 11). Trim HSTs to 2½" x 2½" for throw, 3" x 3" for twin, and 4" x 4" for queen.

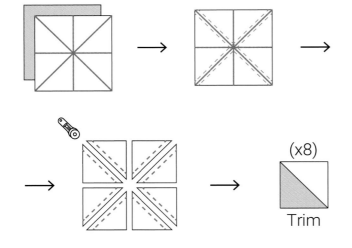

(x8)

Trim

Block One

1. Create (3) rows. The first row is (1) **Light HST**, (1) **Dark HST**, and (2) **Light HSTs**, as shown in *Diagram 1*, Row 1. Press seams to the right.

DIAGRAM 1

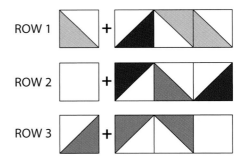

ROW 1 +

ROW 2 +

ROW 3 +

2. The second row is (1) **H** piece, (1) **Dark HST**, (1) **Medium HST**, and (1) **Dark HST**, as shown in *Diagram 1*, Row 2. Press seams to the left.

3. The third row is (3) **Medium HST** and (1) **H** piece, as shown in *Diagram 1*, Row 3. Press seams to the right.

4. Sew the rows together, nesting your seams as you go. Press seams down. Make (3) of these blocks.

Block Two

1. Create (4) columns. The first column is (1) **Light HST**, (1) **H** piece, and (1) **Medium HST**, as shown in *Diagram 2*, Column 1. Press seams up.

DIAGRAM 2

Columns:

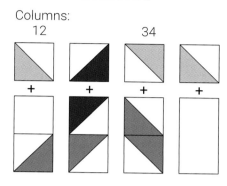

2. The second column is (2) **Dark HSTs** and (1) **Medium HST**, as shown in *Diagram 2*, Column 2. Press seams down.

3. The third column is (1) **Light HST** and (2) **Medium HSTs**, as shown in *Diagram 2*, Column 3. Press seams up.

4. The fourth column is (1) **Light HST** and (1) **G** piece, as shown in *Diagram 2*, Column 4. Press seams down.

5. Sew the columns together, nesting your seams as you go. Press seams to the left. Make (1) of these blocks.

Block Three

1. Create (4) columns. The first column is (1) **G** piece and (1) **Medium HST**, as shown in *Diagram 3*, Column 1. Press seams up.

DIAGRAM 3

Columns:

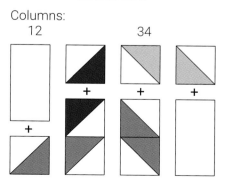

2. The second column is (2) **Dark HSTs** and (1) **Medium HST**, as shown in *Diagram 3*, Column 2. Press seams down.

3. The third column is (1) **Light HST** and (2) **Medium HSTs**, as shown in *Diagram 3*, Column 3. Press seams up.

4. The fourth column is (1) **Light HST** and (1) **G** piece, as shown in *Diagram 3*, Column 4. Press seams down.

5. Sew the columns together, nesting your seams as you go. Press seams to the right. Make (11) of these blocks.

Block Four

1. Create (4) columns. The first column is (1) **H** piece, (1) **Light HST**, and (1) **Medium HST**, as shown in *Diagram 4*, Column 1. Press seams up.

DIAGRAM 4

Columns:

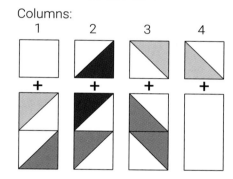

2. The second column is (2) **Dark HSTs** and (1) **Medium HST**, as shown in *Diagram 4*, Column 2. Press seams down.

3. The third column is (1) **Light HST** and (2) **Medium HSTs**, as shown in *Diagram 4*, Column 3. Press seams up.

4. The fourth column is (1) **Light HST** and (1) **G** piece, as shown in *Diagram 4*, Column 4. Press seams down.

5. Sew the columns together, nesting your seams as you go. Press seams to the right. Make (2) of these blocks.

Block Five

1. Create (3) rows. The first row is (1) **H** piece, (1) **Dark HST**, and (2) **Medium HSTs**, as shown in *Diagram 5*, Row 1. Press seams to the right.

DIAGRAM 5

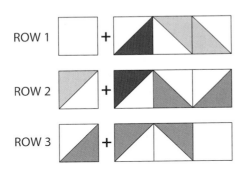

2. The second row is (1) **Light HST**, (1) **Dark HST**, and (2) **Medium HSTs**, as shown in *Diagram 5*, Row 2. Press seams to the left.

3. The third row is (3) **Medium HSTs** and (1) **H** piece, as shown in *Diagram 5*, Row 3. Press seams to the right.

4. Sew the rows together, nesting your seams as you go. Press seams up. Make (1) of these blocks.

Block Six

1. Create (2) rows. The first row is (1) **H** piece, (1) **Dark HST**, (1) **Medium HST**, and (1) **Light HST**, as shown in *Diagram 6*, Row 1. Press seams to the right.

DIAGRAM 6

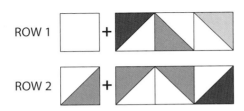

2. The second row is (3) **Medium HSTs** and (1) **Dark HST**, as shown in *Diagram 6*, Row 2. Press seams to the left.

3. Sew the rows together, nesting your seams as you go. Press seams up. Make (3) of these blocks.

Blocks Seven to Ten

1. Create (2) columns. The first column is (4) **Dark HSTs**, as shown in *Diagram 7*, Column 1. Press seams down.

DIAGRAM 7   DIAGRAM 8   DIAGRAM 9

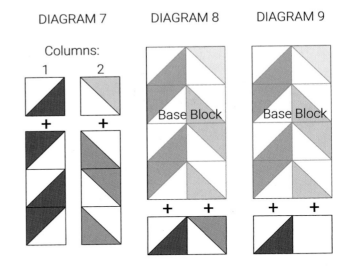

2. The second column is (1) **Light HST** and (3) **Medium HSTs**, as shown in *Diagram 7*, Column 2. Press seams up.

3. Sew the columns together, nesting your seams as you go. Press seams to the right. Make (6) of these blocks. These are the base blocks for Blocks 7–10.

4. Sew together (1) **Dark HST** and (1) **Medium HST**, as shown in *Diagram 8*, and press to the left. Sew to the bottom of the base block. Press seams. Make (1) of these. This is Block 7.

5. Sew together (1) **Dark HST** and (1) **H** piece, as shown in *Diagram 9*, and press to the left. Sew to the bottom of the base block. Press seams. Make (2) of these. These are Block 8.

6. Sew together (1) **Light HST** and (1) **F** piece, as shown in *Diagram 10*. Press up. Make (3) of these columns. Sew one to the right side of each Block 7 and Block 8. Sew (1) **E** piece to the left side of each Block 7 and 8. Press seams to the right.

8. The second column is (2) **Medium HSTs** and (1) **H** piece, as shown in *Diagram 11*, Column 2. Press seams up. Sew the two columns together and press to one side. Sew this section to the bottom of the base block. Make (1) of these. This is Block 9.

DIAGRAM 10

Block 7 (x1)

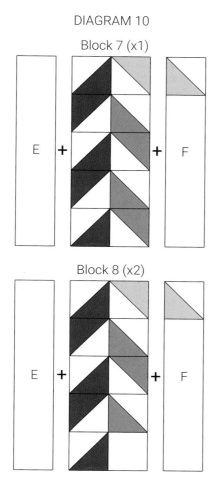

Block 8 (x2)

DIAGRAM 11   DIAGRAM 12

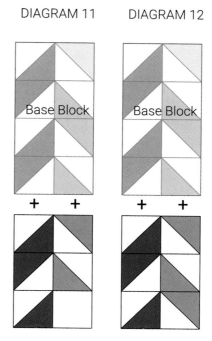

9. Create (2) columns. The first column is (3) **Dark HSTs**, as shown in *Diagram 12*, Column 1. Press seams down.

10. The second column is (3) **Medium HSTs**, as shown in *Diagram 12*, Column 2. Press seams up. Sew the two columns together and press to one side. Sew this section to the bottom of the base block. Make (2) of these. This is Block 10.

7. Create (2) columns. The first column is (3) **Dark HSTs**, as shown in *Diagram 11*, Column 1. Press seams down.

11. Sew together (1) **Light HST** and (1) **D** piece, as shown in *Diagram 13*. Press up. Make (3) of these columns. Sew one to the right side of each Block 9 and Block 10. Sew (1) **C** piece to the left side of each Block 9 and 10. Press seams to the right.

DIAGRAM 13

Block 9 (x1)

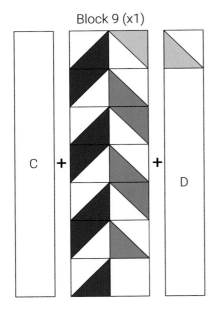

Block 10 (x2)

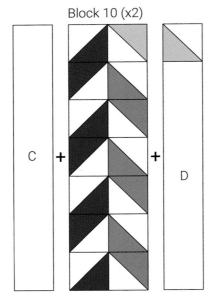

Blocks Eleven to Sixteen

1. Sew together (1) **H** piece and (1) **Medium HST**, as shown in *Diagram 14*. Press toward the **H** piece. Make (17) of these.

DIAGRAM 14

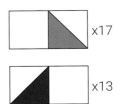

x17

x13

2. Sew together (1) **Dark HST** and (1) **H** piece, as shown in *Diagram 15*. Press toward the **H** piece. Make (13) of these.

DIAGRAM 15

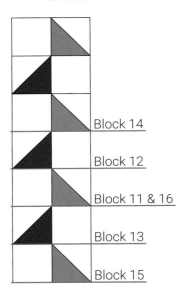

Block 14

Block 12

Block 11 & 16

Block 13

Block 15

3. Make (6) columns, one each for Blocks 11–16. Each block has a different number of rows. See *Diagram 15* for how many rows each block needs.

4. Starting with (1) **Medium HST** row, sew rows together, alternating between the medium and dark colored rows. Press seams down.

5. Finish assembling Blocks 11–16 by sewing the bottom piece (if it has one) and press down. Add the side strips and press to one side.

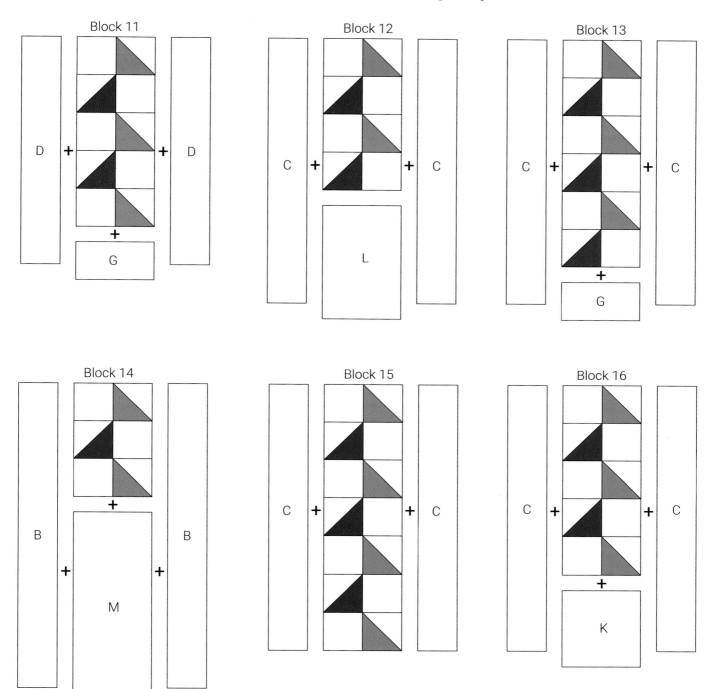

Assembling the Quilt Top

1. Assemble columns using the blocks as shown. Press the seams in each column in the opposite direction as the last one. Sew the columns together and press the seams to one side.

2. Sew the **J** piece to the bottom of the quilt top and press seam down.

BLOCK 1	BLOCK 6	BLOCK 1	BLOCK 6	BLOCK 1	BLOCK 6
BLOCK 2	BLOCK 4B	BLOCK 3	LOCK 4	BLOCK 3	BLOCK 5
BLOCK 3	BLOCK 3	BLOCK 3	BLOCK 3	BLOCK 3	BLOCK 3
BLOCK 3	BLOCK 3	BLOCK 10	BLOCK 9	BLOCK 10	BLOCK 3
BLOCK 7	BLOCK 8B				LOCK 8
BLOCK 11	BLOCK 12	BLOCK 13	BLOCK 14	BLOCK 15	BLOCK 16

3. Create (2) side columns. Column one is (1) **Light HST**, (1) **Dark HST**, (1) **H** piece, (1) **Light HST**, (1) **G** piece, (1) **Light HST**, and (1) **A** piece as shown. Press seams down.

4. Column two is (1) **Light HST**, (1) **G** piece, (1) **Medium HST**, (1) **G** piece, (1) **Light HST**, and (1) **A** piece as shown. Press seams down. Sew column one to the left of the quilt top and column two to the right of the quilt top. Press seams. Quilt and bind.

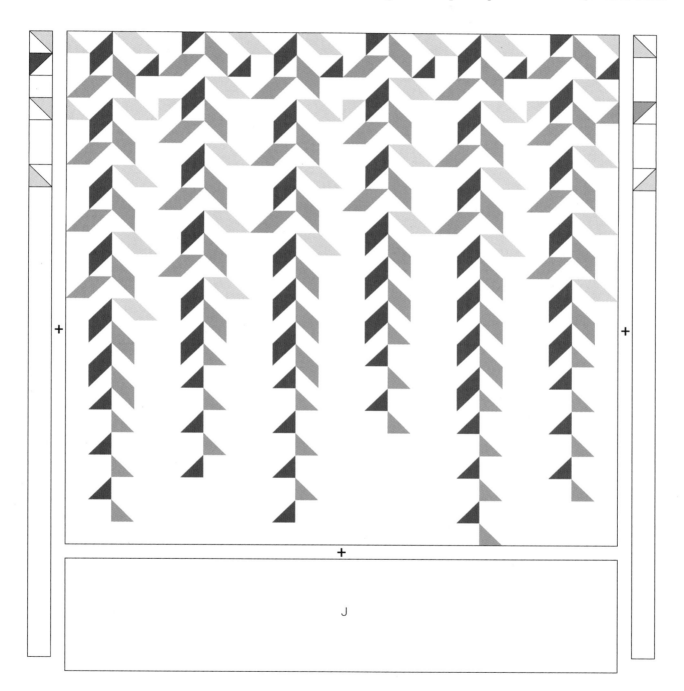

J

Intro to Flying Geese

The **Flying Geese** block is another one of those foundational blocks that every quilter should know how to do. It is basically just another variation of HSTs, which overlap on the same block. You can also make a bunch of these from scraps and put them together to see what kind of design you come up with.

A Flying Geese block is made up of a base rectangle and two squares. The typical ratio for the rectangle is 1:2. The two side pieces are a 1:1 ratio. For example, the rectangle piece would be 2" x 4" with each of your side pieces being 2" x 2".

Traditional Method

Place one of the squares on the end of the rectangle with RST. Mark a diagonal line. Sew on the diagonal. Trim off the excess and press the seam to one side. Do the same on the other side of the rectangle. You will have one Flying Geese block.

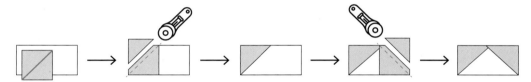

"No-Waste" Method

You can also make four sets of Flying Geese at once by using this technique.

Draw two diagonal lines on the back of your base square and a diagonal line on the backs of each of the four smaller squares. Align two smaller squares on the diagonal line of the larger square and with its corners. The two smaller squares will slightly overlap in the center. Sew ¼" on both sides of this line.

Cut on the line and press the squares open. Add the remaining squares on each of the remaining diagonal lines of the larger square. Sew on both sides of the line. Cut on the line for both squares. You will have four Flying Geese. Always make sure to trim your Flying Geese before using them in a quilt to ensure accuracy.

Let's use this traditional foundation block in some modern quilts and projects!

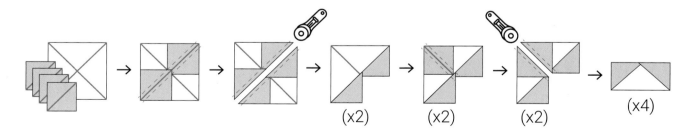

Gaggle Pincushion & Thrashcan

I always find myself searching my quilt room for where I last left my box of pins. This long, skinny pincushion is meant to sit in front of your sewing machine or along the side. Its slim profile keeps it out of the way while also staying close by for accessibility. It's my favorite pincushion! Another handy item is the "thrashcan," named because it is a trashcan for thread. Keep this near your sewing machine for an easy way to prevent messes in your work area.

Before You Start

Read through all the directions and steps before you start. All seams are sewn with a ¼" seam allowance.

For more inspiration, check out the hashtags #gagglepincushion, #gagglethrashcan, and #kileysquiltroom. Be sure to use these when you post pictures of your quilt to share with others!

WOF = Width of Fabric
RST = Right Sides Together
FQ = Fat Quarter

FABRIC REQUIREMENTS

	Pincushion & Thrashcan
Color 1	1 FQ
Color 2	1 FQ
Background	¼ yard or 1 FQ
Accent/Lining	1 FQ

Supplies

Bag of crushed walnut shells or polyester fiberfill
(2) 5¼" x 6¼" fusible fleece
(2) 5" x 6" lightweight interfacing
Disappearing fabric pen

CUTTING INSTRUCTIONS

	Pincushion & Thrashcan
Color 1	(1) 3¼" x 3¼" (1) 4¼" x 4¼"
Color 2	(1) 3¼" x 3¼" (1) 4¼" x 4¼"
Background	(8) 1⅞" x 1⅞" (8) 2⅜" x 2⅜" (1) 1" x 3½" (1) 1¾" x 3½" (1) 5¼" x 6¼" (1) 1½" x 6¼"
Accent/Lining	(1) 3½" x 9½" (2) 5" x 6" (1) 2" x 4"

Flying Geese

1. Draw two diagonal lines on the front of all your Color 1 and Color 2 squares. Draw one diagonal line on the back of all your background squares.

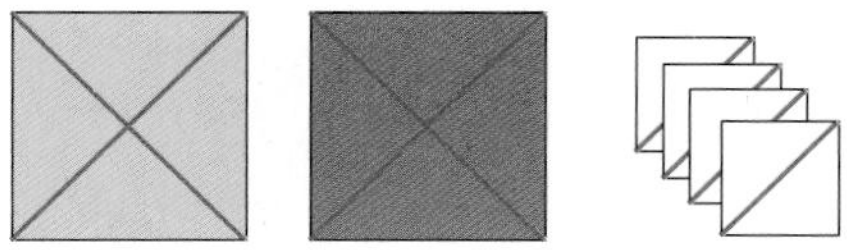

2. Align (2) 2⅜" x 2⅜" background squares with the diagonal line of (1) 4¼" x 4¼" Color 1 square and its corners, as shown. Sew ¼" on both sides of this line. Cut on the line and press the squares open.

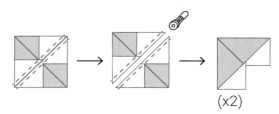

(x2)

3. Add (1) 2⅜" x 2⅜" background square on each of the remaining diagonal lines of the Color 1 square. Sew on both sides of the line and cut. You will have four Flying Geese. Trim each to 2" x 3½".

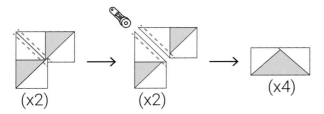

4. Repeat steps 2–3 with the 4¼" x 4¼" Color 2 square. Set aside for the **Gaggle Pincushion**.

5. Align (2) 1⅞" x 1⅞" background squares with the diagonal line of (1) 3¼" x 3¼" Color 1 square and its corners, as shown. Sew ¼" on both sides of this line. Cut on the line and press the squares open.

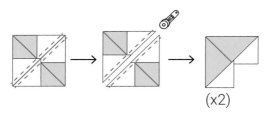

6. Add (1) 1⅞" x 1⅞" background square on each of the remaining diagonal lines of the Color 1 square. Sew on both sides of the line and cut. You will have four Flying Geese. Trim each to 1½" x 2½".

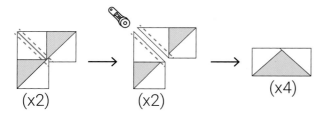

7. Repeat steps 5–6 with the 3¼" x 3¼" Color 2 square. Set aside for the **Gaggle Thrashcan**.

Gaggle Pincushion

1. Sew together (3) Color 1 Flying Geese and (3) Color 2 Flying Geese, alternating colors as shown. Press seams to one side.

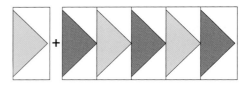

2. Lay this unit on top of a 3½" x 9½" accent piece, RST. Sew all the way around the edges, leaving a 2" gap on an end for flipping and filling the piece.

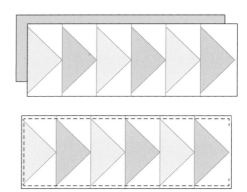

3. Flip the piece right side out and press the edges. Fill with crushed walnut pieces or stuffing. Carefully top stitch your opening closed (hand stitched is the preferred method for an invisible seam). Now your Gaggle Pincushion is ready to be used right away!

Gaggle Thrashcan

1. Sew together (2) rows of Flying Geese. The first row is Color 1, Color 2, and Color 1. The second row is Color 2, Color 1, and Color 2. Press both rows toward the direction that the Flying Geese are pointing. Flip the second row to face the opposite direction and sew the rows together, pressing the seam open. Your block should measure 3½" x 4½".

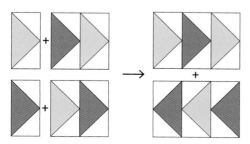

2. Sew the 1" x 3½" background piece to the top of your Flying Geese block. Sew the 1¾" x 3½" background piece to the bottom of your Flying Geese block. Press seams toward the background pieces.

3. Sew the (2) 1½" x 6¼" background pieces both sides of the block. Press seams toward the background pieces. Your block should now measure 5¼" x 6¼".

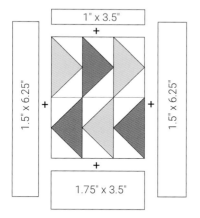

4. Follow manufacturer instructions to adhere the fusible fleece to the **wrong sides** of the Flying Geese block and the 5¼" x 6¼" background piece. Apply the lightweight interfacing to the wrong side of the (2) 5" x 6" accent fabric panels.

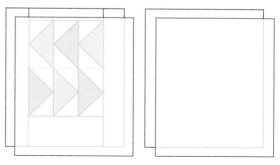

Exterior panels with fusible fleece on the backs

Interior panels with fusible interfacing on the backs

TIP

Attach a removable hook to the front or side of your sewing machine to hang your thrashcan from. Now it is ready for your next project!

5. Place one exterior panel right side up. Using a disappearing fabric pen, mark a ¾" x ¾" square on both bottom corners, as shown. Using scissors, cut along the marked lines. Repeat on the 5" x 6" accent fabric panels.

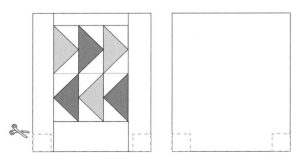

Exterior panels

Interior panels

6. Place exterior panels RST and pin or clip the bottom edge in place. Stitch along the bottom edge. Press seams open. Use a ⅛" seam allowance and stitch along each side of the seam, attaching the seam allowance to the panels. Repeat with your interior panels.

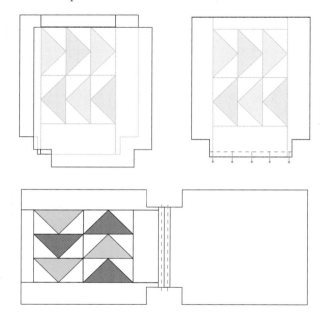

7. Bring exterior panels right sides together again. Align and clip side edges. Stitch along each side, backstitching at the beginning and end. Press the seam open. Repeat with your interior panels.

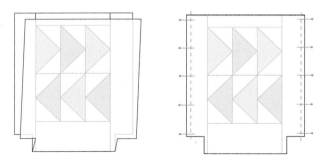

8. Align one side seam over the bottom seam to stitch the boxed corner of your thrashcan closed. Pin or clip in place. Sew, backstitching at the beginning and end. Repeat process for the other corner. Turn assembled thrashcan exterior right side out. Repeat with your interior panels.

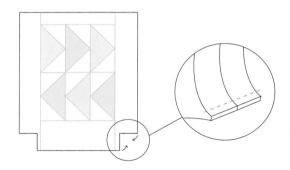

Hanging Tab (Optional)

1. On the 2" x 4" accent fabric, press wrong sides together lengthwise. Open the fabric, align the raw edges with the middle crease, and press. Press in half lengthwise again. Use pins or clips to hold the folded edge closed and top stitch along the open edge.

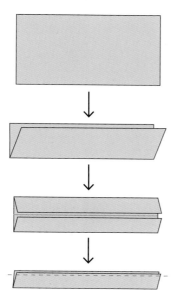

2. With the exterior thrashcan right side out, use a disappearing pen to mark the center of the back panel along the top edge. Align the raw ends of the tab with the top of the thrashcan on both sides of the mark, as shown. Pin or clip the ends in place, making sure not to twist the handle. Sew in place using an ⅛" seam allowance.

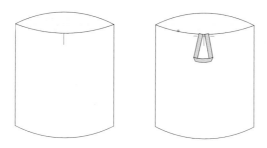

Assembling the Thrashcan

1. Insert finished exterior inside interior, RST. Align side seams with the top raw edges of the exterior and lining. Clip into place. Make sure the hanging tab is pushed down between the two layers. This may be tricky because the lining is smaller than the exterior, but keep working with it and use lots of clips or pins. Stitch around the top of the thrashcan, making sure to leave a 3" gap for turning.

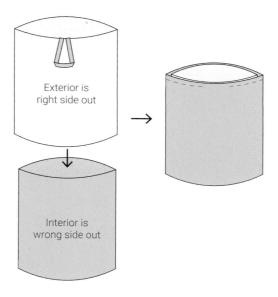

Exterior is right side out

Interior is wrong side out

2. Turn the thrashcan right side out through the opening in the top seam. Roll the seam between your fingers to make it as neat as possible and press. Clip or pin all the way around the top of the thrashcan, closing the opening used for turning. Top stitch around the top edge using both an ⅛" seam allowance and a ¼" seam allowance, backstitching at the beginning and end. Trim off any extra threads.

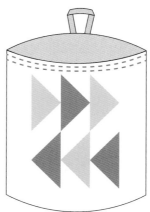

Runway Quilt

This design is a great example of mixing a traditional block, like a Flying Geese, and modern clean lines to get something new and exciting! When I designed this pattern, I was immediately reminded of all the runways at airports. My husband has spent the past two years studying and practicing to get his private pilot's license. Now that he has it, it has been a great blessing to our family because we get to take the kids flying and even go out alone for date nights. Such a fun experience! I knew I wanted this quilt to reflect all those good times we have had and are yet to come with my husband's new hobby.

Before You Start

Read through all the directions and steps before you start. All seams are sewn with a ¼" seam allowance.

For more inspiration, check out the hashtag #riverbendquilt and #kileysquiltroom. Be sure to use these when you post pictures of your quilt to share with others!

WOF = Width of Fabric
RST = Right Sides Together

FABRIC REQUIREMENTS

	Throw 60" x 62½"	Twin 66" x 87¼"	Queen 90" x 96¼"
Colors 1–8	½ yard each	½ yard each	¾ yard each
Background	1¾ yards	3¼ yards	3½ yards
Backing	3¾ yard	6 yards	8½ yards
Binding	½ yard	¾ yard	1 yard

CUTTING INSTRUCTIONS

	Throw 60" x 62½"	Twin 66" x 87¼"	Queen 90" x 96¼"
Background	(13) 3" x WOF, sew end to end, subcut: (9) 3" x 60½" **F** (5) 3" x WOF, subcut: (16) 3" x 5½" **J** (32) 3" x 3" **K**	(5) 3¼" x WOF, subcut: (16) 3¼" x 6" **J** (32) 3¼" x 3¼" **K** (12) 3¼" x WOF, sew end to end, subcut: (7) 3¼" x 66½" **F** (4) 12½" x WOF, sew end to end, subcut: (2) 12½" x 66½" **G**	(6) 4¼" x WOF, subcut: (16) 4¼" x 8" **J** (32) 4¼" x 4¼" **K** (16) 4¼" x WOF, sew end to end, subcut: (7) 4¼" x 90½" **F** (5) 5½" x WOF, sew end to end, subcut: (2) 5½" x 90½" **G**

Color 1	(2) 5½" x WOF, subcut: (1) 5½" x 30½" **1D** (1) 5½" x 20½" **1C** (2) 5½" x 3" **1A** (4) 3" x 3" **1B**	(2) 6" x WOF, subcut: (1) 6" x 33½" **1D** (1) 6" x 22½" **1C** (2) 6" x 3¼" **1A** (4) 3¼" x 3¼" **1B**	(3) 8" x WOF, sew end to end, subcut: (1) 8" x 45½" **1D** (1) 8" x 30½" **1C** (2) 8" x 4¼" **1A** (4) 4¼" x 4¼" **1B**
Color 2	(2) 5½" x WOF, subcut: (1) 5½" x 28½" **2D** (1) 5½" x 10½" **2C** (1) 5½" x 7½" **2E** (3) 5½" x 3" **2A** (6) 3" x 3" **2B**	(2) 6" x WOF, subcut: (1) 6" x 31½" **2D** (1) 6" x 11½ **2C** (1) 6" x 8" **2E** (3) 6" x 3¼" **2A** (6) 3¼" x 3¼" **2B**	(3) 8" x WOF, sew end to end, subcut: (1) 8" x 42½" **2D** (1) 8" x 15½" **2C** (1) 8" x 11" **2E** (3) 8" x 4¼" **2A** (6) 4¼" x 4¼" **2B**
Color 3	(2) 5½" x WOF, subcut: (1) 5½" x 33½" **3C** (1) 5½" x 22½" **3D** (1) 5½" x 3" **3A** (2) 3" x 3" **3B**	(2) 6" x WOF, subcut: (1) 6" x 37" **3C** (1) 6" x 24½" **3D** (1) 6" x 3¼" **3A** (2) 3¼" x 3¼" **3B**	(3) 8" x WOF, sew end to end, subcut: (1) 8" x 50" **3C** (1) 8" x 33½" **3D** (1) 8" x 4¼" **3A** (2) 4¼" x 4¼" **3B**
Color 4	(2) 5½" x WOF, subcut: (1) 5½" x 37½" **4D** (1) 5½" x 13½" **4C** (2) 5½" x 3" **4A** (4) 3" x 3" **4B**	(2) 6" x WOF, subcut: (1) 6" x 41" **4D** (1) 6" x 15" **4C** (2) 6" x 3¼" **4A** (4) 3¼" x 3¼" **4B**	(3) 8" x WOF, sew end to end, subcut: (1) 8" x 56" **4D** (1) 8" x 20" **4C** (2) 8" x 4¼" **4A** (4) 4¼" x 4¼" **4B**
Color 5	(2) 5½" x WOF, subcut: (1) 5½" x 25½" **5C** (1) 5½" x 12½" **5E** (1) 5½" x 8½" **5D** (3) 5½" x 3" **5A** (6) 3" x 3" **5B**	(2) 6" x WOF, subcut: (1) 6" x 28" **5C** (1) 6" x 13½" **5E** (1) 6" x 9½" **5D** (3) 6" x 3¼" **5A** (6) 3¼" x 3¼" **5B**	(3) 8" x WOF, sew end to end, subcut: (1) 8" x 38" **5C** (1) 8" x 18½" **5E** (1) 8" x 12½" **5D** (3) 8" x 4¼" **5A** (6) 4¼" x 4¼" **5B**
Color 6	(2) 5½" x WOF, sew end to end, subcut: (1) 5½" x 47½" **6D** (1) 5½" x 8½" **6C** (1) 5½" x 3" **6A** (2) 3" x 3" **6B**	(2) 6" x WOF, sew end to end, subcut: (1) 6" x 52½" **6C** (1) 6" x 9" **6D** (1) 6" x 3¼" **6A** (2) 3¼" x 3¼" **6B**	(3) 8" x WOF, sew end to end, subcut: (1) 8" x 80" **6C** (1) 8" x 12½" **6D** (1) 8" x 4¼" **6A** (2) 4¼" x 4¼" **6B**
Color 7	(2) 5½" x WOF, subcut: (1) 5½" x 8½" **7E** (1) 5½" x 16½" **7D** (1) 5½" x 21½" **7C** (3) 5½" x 3" **7A** (6) 3" x 3" **7B**	(2) 6" x WOF, subcut: (1) 6" x 9½" **7E** (1) 6" x 18" **7D** (1) 6" x 23½" **7C** (3) 6" x 3¼" **7A** (6) 3¼" x 3¼" **7B**	(3) 8" x WOF, sew end to end, subcut: (1) 8" x 12½" **7E** (1) 8" x 24½" **7D** (1) 8" x 32" **7C** (3) 8" x 4¼" **7A** (6) 4¼" x 4¼" **7B**
Color 8	(2) 5½" x WOF, subcut: (1) 5½" x 18½" **8D** (1) 5½" x 37½" **8C** (1) 5½" x 3" **8A** (2) 3" x 3" **8B**	(2) 6" x WOF, subcut: (1) 6" x 20½" **8D** (1) 6" x 41" **8C** (1) 6" x 3¼" **8A** (2) 3¼" x 3¼" **8B**	(3) 8" x WOF, sew end to end, subcut: (1) 8" x 27½" **8D** (1) 8" x 56" **8C** (1) 8" x 4¼" **8A** (2) 4¼" x 4¼" **8B**

Flying Geese

1. Draw diagonal lines on the backs of all **1B** through **8B** pieces. Draw a diagonal line on the backs of the **K** pieces.

2. Place (1) **1B–8B** piece on one end of each **J** piece with RST. Sew on the diagonal. Trim off the excess and press the seam to one side. Do the same on the other side of the rectangle. Trim to 3" x 5½". Label these as **1BB–8BB**.

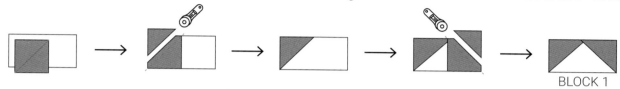

BLOCK 1

3. Place (1) **K** piece on one end of each **1A–8A** piece with RST. Sew on the diagonal. Trim off the excess and press the seam to one side. Do the same on the other side of the rectangle. Trim to 3" x 5½". Label these as **1AA–8AA**.

BLOCK 2

Making the Rows

1. **Row 1**: Sew together the labeled pieces as shown. Press all the seams to one side.

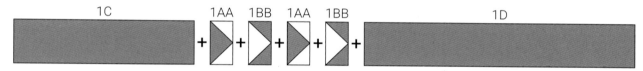

2. **Row 2**: Sew together the labeled pieces as shown. Press all the seams to one side.

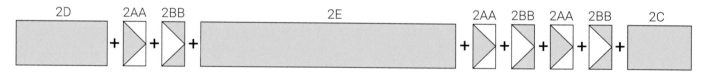

3. **Row 3**: Sew together the labeled pieces as shown. Press all the seams to one side.

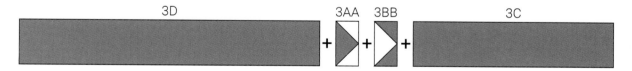

4. **Row 4**: Sew together the labeled pieces as shown. Press all the seams to one side.

5. **Row 5**: Sew together the labeled pieces as shown. Press all the seam to one side.

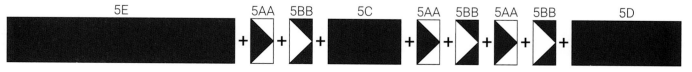

6. **Row 6**: Sew together the labeled pieces as shown. Press all the seams to one side.

7. **Row 7**: Sew together the labeled pieces as shown. Press all the seams to one side.

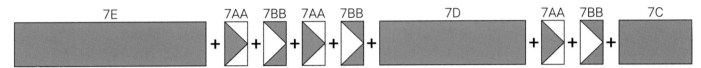

8. **Row 8**: Sew together the labeled pieces as shown. Press all the seams to one side.

Assembling the Quilt Top

1. Sew together the labeled rows as shown. Press all the seams in the same direction. Quilt and bind.

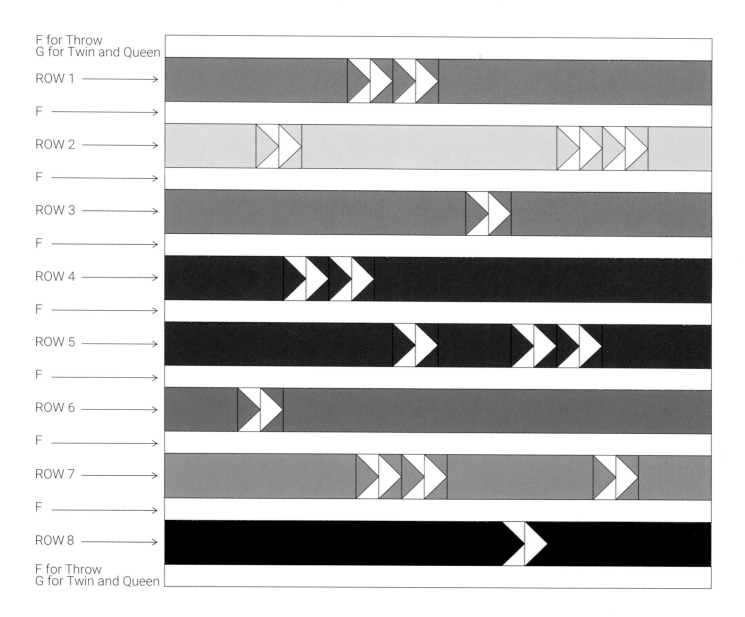

F for Throw
G for Twin and Queen

ROW 1 ⟶

F ⟶

ROW 2 ⟶

F ⟶

ROW 3 ⟶

F ⟶

ROW 4 ⟶

F ⟶

ROW 5 ⟶

F ⟶

ROW 6 ⟶

F ⟶

ROW 7 ⟶

F ⟶

ROW 8 ⟶

F for Throw
G for Twin and Queen

Intro to Curved Piecing

There are several different ways to create **curves** in quilts. If you've ever sewn garments, it is very similar to sewing sleeves into the bodice. There are three basic techniques. We will go over them from easiest to hardest. Keep in mind that the smaller the circle, the tighter the curve and the trickier it is to sew.

Quarter Circle

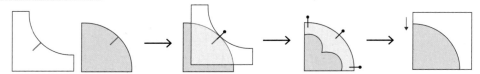

The easiest is the quarter circle, also known as the "Drunkard's Path." Another one of those classic foundational blocks!

Pinch your frame piece and quarter-circle piece in half to create a crease at the center. With RST and curves facing opposite directions, align the center creases and pin. Force the curve of the frame to follow the curve of the quarter circle, and pin the ends. Slowly sew together, keeping edges aligned. Press toward the inside of the curve.

Half Circle

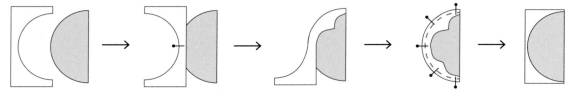

The next step up is the half circle. It is all the same steps, but taking the curve further. Go slowly to keep fabric steady and clear of puckers.

Inset Circle

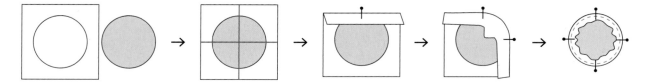

The most technically advanced curve is the inset circle. But if you have the other two curves down, this one won't be as hard as it looks! It just takes practice.

You have your "frame" and your "inner circle." Fold in half twice, pressing for each. Lay the frame on top of the inner circle, both pieces right side up, aligning the creases in the fabrics.

Beginning with the top edge of the frame piece, pull the edge down toward the center until the edges of both curves are aligned (now they are RST). Pin in place where the creases match. Do this same thing on all sides on the creases. The entire frame should now be facing down. Sew a ¼" seam allowance around the circle, aligning the edges as you go. Press toward the center.

Mod Curve Pillows

Makes two 20" x 20" pillowcases

I love a good weekend project to break up my big quilt tops! These pillows add some modern flare to your living room or bedroom.

Before You Start

Read through all the directions and steps before you start. All seams are sewn with a ¼" seam allowance. **All templates need to be printed at 100%** and *not* "fit to page." You can adjust this in your printer settings. Verify that your template is printed at the correct size by measuring all sides of the 1" reference square.

For more inspiration, check out the hashtag #quiltedmodpillows and #kileysquiltroom. Be sure to use these when you post pictures of your quilt to share with others!

WOF = Width of Fabric
FQ = Fat Quarter
WST = Wrong Sides Together
RST = Right Sides Together

Supplies

Templates (pages 117–122)
(2) 22" x 22" pillow forms
No-sew Velcro or button (optional)

FABRIC REQUIREMENTS

Color 1	Color 2	Color 3	Color 4	Backing	Binding
¼ yard	1 yard	1 FQ	1 FQ	1½ yards	½ yard

CUTTING INSTRUCTIONS

Color 1	Color 2	Color 3	Color 4
(2) 2" x WOF, subcut: (1) 2" x 5½" (1) 2" x 7½" (1) 2" x 9" (1) 2" x 10½" (1) 2" x 10¾" (1) 2" x 15½" (1) 2" x 20½"	(2) 2" x WOF, subcut: (2) 2" x 5½" (1) 2" x 3½" (3) 2" x 10½" (2) 2" x 20½" (1) 3½" x WOF, subcut: (1) 3½" x 20½" (1) 9½" x WOF, subcut: (1) 9" x 9" (1) 9" x 10½" (1) 11" x WOF, subcut: (1) 11" x 18" (1) 10" x 20½"	(2) 8" x 15"	(1) 6½" x 9" (1) 6½" x 8" (1) 6¼" x 10¾" (1) 3½" x 10¾"

Pillow One

1. Sew (1) 2" x 15½" Color 1 strip to (1) 2" x 5½" Color 2 strip. Press to the dark side. This is **Strip A**.

2. Sew (1) 2" x 10½" Color 1 strip to (1) 2" x 10½" Color 2 strip. Press to the dark side. This is **Strip B**.

3. Sew a set of strips as directed, pressing seams down.

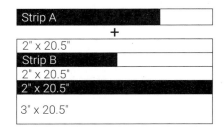

4. Align the corner of *Template A* with the lower-right corner of this strip set. Cut along the curve.

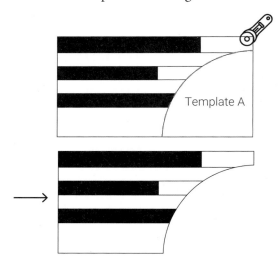

5. Sew another strip set made of (1) 6¼" x 10¾" Color 4 piece, (1) 2" x 10¾" Color 1 piece, and (1) 3½" x 10¾" Color 4 piece. Press seams up. Align the corner of *Template B* with the bottom-right corner of this strip set. Cut along the curve.

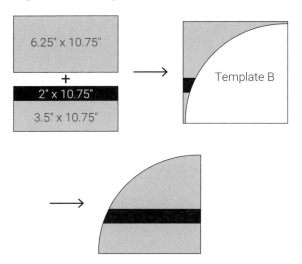

6. Mark the centers of each curve with a crease. With RST, pin the creases and ends together using the quarter-circle method (page 38). Sew along the curve. Press seams toward the bottom-right corner. It should measure 11" x 20½". Set aside.

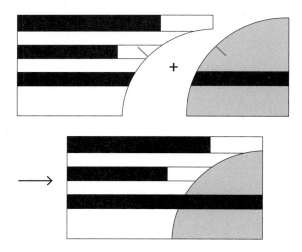

7. Place the straight edge of *Template C* along a long edge of the 8" x 15" Color 3 piece. Cut along the curve.

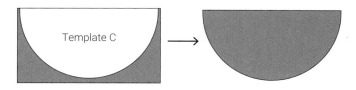

8. Along one of the long edges of the 10" x 20½" Color 2 piece, mark ½" from the end. Place the straight edge of *Template D* along this edge with one of the ends at the mark. Cut along the curve.

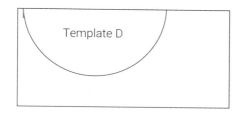

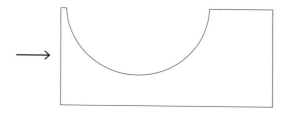

9. Sew the Color 3 semicircle into the Color 2 piece using the half-circle method (page 38). Press toward the semicircle. Trim to 10" x 20½".

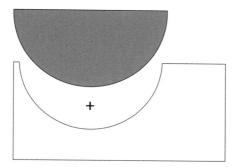

10. Sew this section above the section from step 6. Press seam to one side. It should measure 20½" x 20½". The top for Pillow One is complete. Set it aside to quilt and assemble into a pillow later.

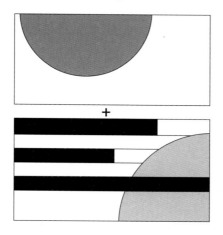

Pillow Two

1. Sew (1) 2" x 3½" Color 2 piece to the left side of (1) 2" x 7½" Color 1 piece. Press to the darker side. Sew (1) 2" x 10½" Color 2 piece to the top of this unit. Press seams. This is **Section A**.

2. Sew (1) 2" x 5½" Color 2 piece to the right side of (1) 2" x 5½" Color 1 piece. Press to the darker side. Sew (1) 2" x 10½" Color 2 piece to the bottom of this unit. Press seams. This is **Section B**.

3. Sew (1) 2" x 9" Color 1 piece to the bottom of (1) 9" x 9" Color 2 square. Press toward the dark side. Sew this section to the left of (1) 9" x 10½" Color 2 piece. Press seams.

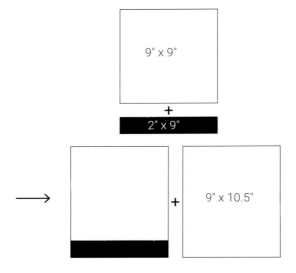

4. Place the straight edge of *Template D* along the long side with the Color 1 strip. Center the template along this bottom edge. Cut along the curve.

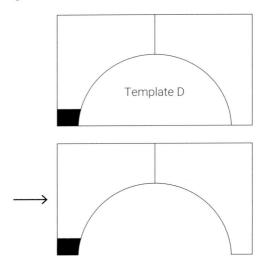

5. Sew (1) 2" x 9" Color 1 piece to the bottom of a 6½" x 9" Color 4 piece. Press toward the dark side. Sew this section to the left of (1) 6½" x 8" Color 4 piece. Press seams.

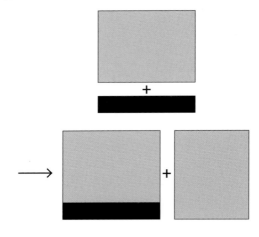

6. Align *Template C* along the middle of the long side with the Color 1 piece on it. Cut along the curve.

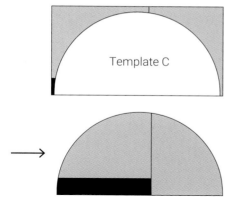

7. Sew the two curves together using the half-circle method. Trim to 10½" x 17½".

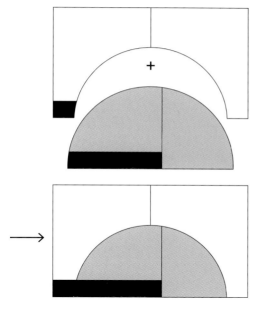

8. Sew **Section B** to the left side of the semicircle block, as shown. Press seams to one side. This is the left half of Pillow Two.

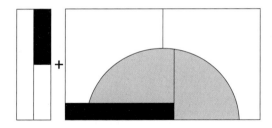

9. Place *Template C* over the 8" x 15" Color 3 piece, centered along a long side. Cut along the curve. Place *Template D* over the 11" x 18" Color 2 piece, centered along a long side. Cut along the curve.

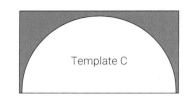

Template C

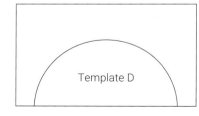

Template D

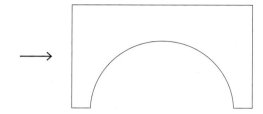

10. Sew the Color 3 curve into the Color 2 curve using the half-circle method. Press to the darker color. Trim to 10½" x 17½".

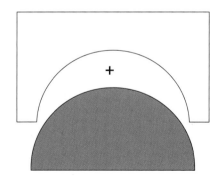

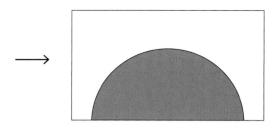

11. Sew **Section A** to the left side of the semicircle block, as shown. Press seams to one side. This is the right half of Pillow Two.

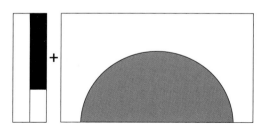

12. Sew the left and right halves of Pillow Two together. Press seams. The pillow top should measure 20½" x 20½".

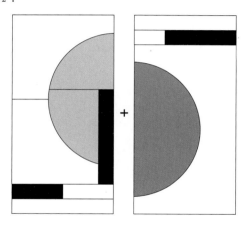

Assembling the Pillows

1. Lay each top on a 22" x 22" piece of batting, or place both next to each other on a 22" x 44" piece of batting. Baste the two layers together and quilt as desired (straight lines, cross hatch, diamonds, improv lines, etc.). Trim excess batting off each pillow top.

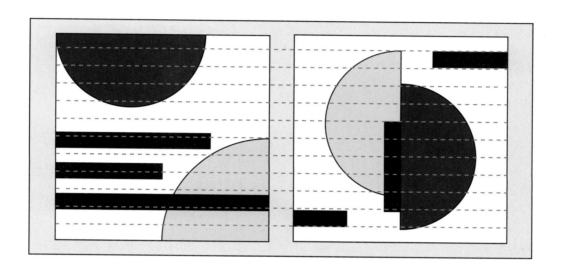

2. Cut (2) 24" strips of backing. From those, cut (4) 24" x 20½" strips. Fold each of these pieces in half so that they now measure 12" x 20½". Lay your pillow front face down. Align the raw edges of one of the backings with the bottom of the pillow front (on the back). Do the same with another backing piece at the top of the pillow. The folded edges of the backing should overlap. Sew ¼" around the entire pillowcase. Repeat for the other pillow top.

3. Bind the edges like you would a quilt. I suggest securing your overlap with some no-sew Velcro or a button. Once you are done, stuff the pillow into your pillowcase.

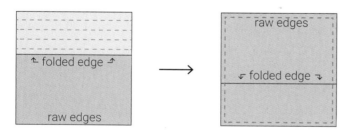

Rope Swing Quilt

Curves are my favorite type of piecing! I love the movement that it brings to a quilt and all the different kinds of shapes you can create. This quilt is made up entirely of Drunkard's Path blocks.

Before You Start

Read through all the directions and steps before you start. All seams are sewn with a ¼" seam allowance. **All templates need to be printed at 100%** and *not* "fit to page." You can adjust this in your printer settings. Verify that your template is printed at the correct size by measuring all sides of the 1" reference square.

For more inspiration, check out the hashtag #ropeswingquilt and #kileysquiltroom. Be sure to use these when you post pictures of your quilt to share with others!

WOF = Width of Fabric
RST = Right Sides Together
HST = Half-Square Triangle

Supplies
Templates (page 111)

FABRIC REQUIREMENTS

	Throw 50" x 60"
Colors 1–5	½ yard each
Background	2¾ yards
Backing	3¼ yards
Binding	½ yard

CUTTING INSTRUCTIONS

	Throw 50" x 60"
Color 1	(2) 5½" x WOF, subcut: (13) 5½" x 5½"
Color 2	(3) 5½" x WOF, subcut: (17) 5½" x 5½"
Color 3	(3) 5½" x WOF, subcut: (21) 5½" x 5½"
Color 4	(3) 5½" x WOF, subcut: (18) 5½" x 5½"
Color 5	(2) 5½" x WOF, subcut: (10) 5½" x 5½"
Background	(11) 5½" x WOF, subcut: (81) 5½" x 5½" A (5) 5½" x WOF, sew end to end and subcut: (2) 5½" x 10½" B (2) 5½" x 15½" C (2) 5½" x 20½" D (1) 5½" x 25½" E (1) 5½" x 35½" F (1) 5½" x 45½" G

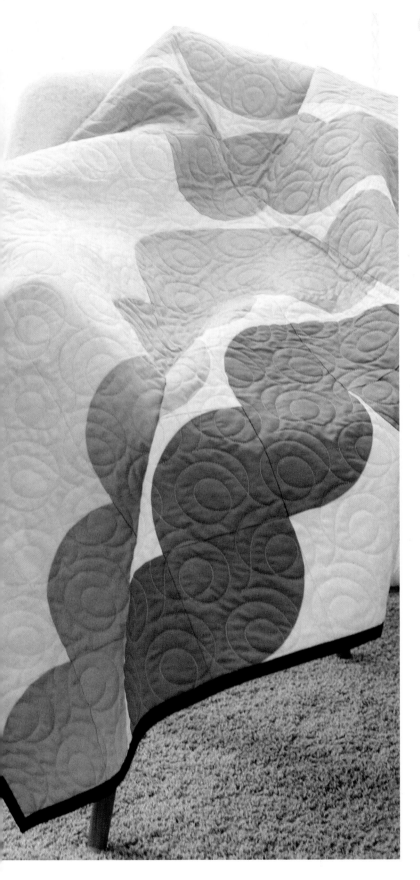

Curves

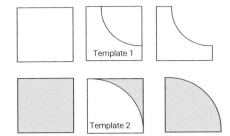

Template 1

Template 2

1. Take (79) **A** pieces and place *Template 1* on top, cutting around the template. This is the frame piece. Take all the 5½" x 5½" color pieces (from all 5 colors) and place *Template 2* on top, cutting around the template. This is the quarter-circle piece.

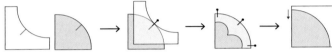

2. Take (1) frame and (1) quarter circle and use the quarter-circle method (page 38). Repeat for all pieces.

x13   x17   x21   x18   x10

3. You will have (13) Color 1 blocks, (17) Color 2 blocks, (21) Color 3 blocks, (18) Color 4 blocks, and (10) Color 5 blocks. Trim each to 5½" x 5½".

Section One

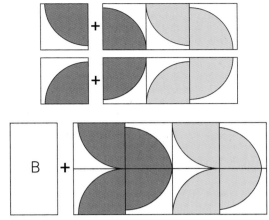

1. Make (2) rows that mirror each other. Sew together (2) Color 1 blocks and (2) Color 2 blocks for each row, arranging as shown. Press the first row to the right and the second row to the left. Sew the rows together, nesting the seams as you go. Press the seam down. Sew (1) **B** piece to the Color 1 end. Press toward the **B** piece.

2. Make (2) more mirroring rows. Sew together (2)

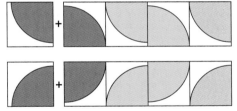

Color 1 blocks, (2) Color 2 blocks, and (1) Color 3 block for each row, as shown.

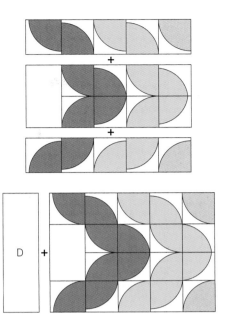

3. Sew the two rows to the top and bottom of the pieced unit, as shown. Press seams down. Sew (1) **D** piece to the Color 1 end. Press toward the **D** piece.

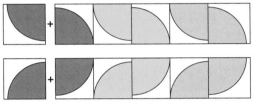

4. Make (2) more mirroring rows. Sew together (2) Color 1 blocks, (2) Color 2 blocks, and (2) Color 3 blocks for each row, as shown.

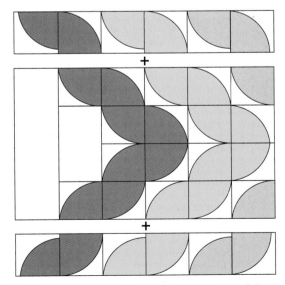

5. Sew the two rows to the top and bottom of the pieced unit, as shown. Press seams down. This is **Section One**. Set aside.

Section Two

1. Sew a row together of (1) Color 1 block, (2) Color 2 blocks, (2) Color 3 blocks, and (1) Color 4 block, as shown. Press seams to the right.

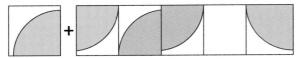

2. Sew a row together of (2) Color 2 blocks, (2) Color 3 blocks, (1) **A** piece, and (1) Color 4 block, as shown. Press seams to the left.

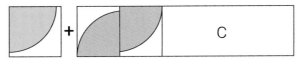

3. Sew a row together of (1) Color 2 blocks, (2) Color 3 blocks, and (1) **C** piece, as shown. Press seams to the right.

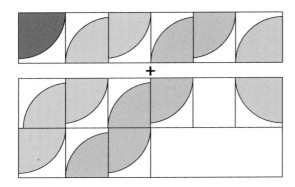

4. Sew the three rows together and press the seams down. This is **Section Two**. Set aside.

Section Three

1. Sew a row together of (1) Color 3 block and (1) **C** piece, as shown. Press seams to the right.

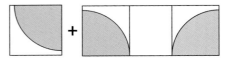

2. Sew a row together of (2) Color 3 blocks, (1) **A** piece, and (1) Color 4 block, as shown. Press seams to the left.

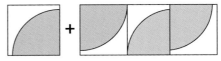

3. Sew a row together of (2) Color 3 blocks and (2) Color 4 blocks, as shown. Press seams to the right.

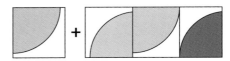

4. Sew a row together of (1) Color 3 block, (2) Color 4 blocks, and (1) Color 5 block, as shown. Press seams to the left.

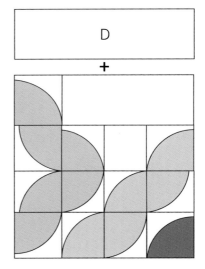

5. Sew the rows together. Sew (1) **D** piece to the top, as shown. Press seams up toward the **D** piece. This is **Section Three**. Set aside.

Section Four

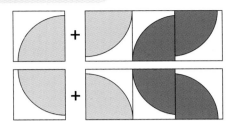

1. Make (2) rows that mirror each other. Sew together (2) Color 4 blocks and (2) Color 5 blocks for each row, as shown. Press seams to the right for the first one and to the left for the second one.

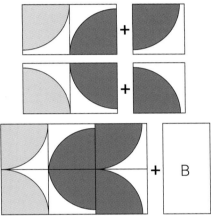

2. Make (2) more mirroring rows. Sew together (1) Color 3 block and (2) Color 4 blocks for each row, as shown. Press seams to the left for the first row and to the right for the second row. Sew the rows together, nesting your seams as you go. Press the seam up. Sew (1) **B** piece to the Color 5 end. Press toward the **B** piece.

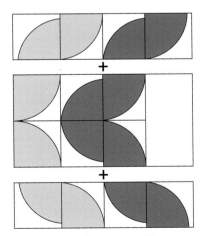

3. Sew the two rows to the top and bottom of the pieced unit, as shown, so that the seam nest. Press seams up. This is **Section Four**. Set aside.

Section Five

1. Sew a row with (2) Color 3 blocks, (1) **E** piece, (2) Color 4 blocks, and (1) Color 5 block as shown. Press seams to the right.

2. Sew a row with (1) Color 3 block, (1) **F** piece, and (2) Color 4 blocks as shown. Press seams to the left.

3. Sew a row with (1) **G** piece and (1) Color 4 block as shown. Press seams to the right.

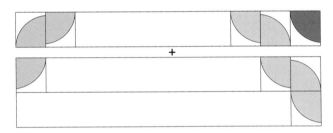

4. Sew the three rows together and press the seams down. This is **Section Five**. Set aside.

Assembling the Quilt Top

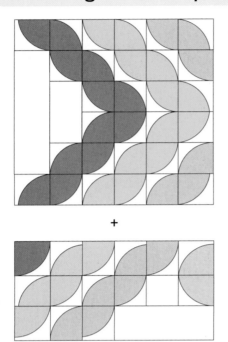

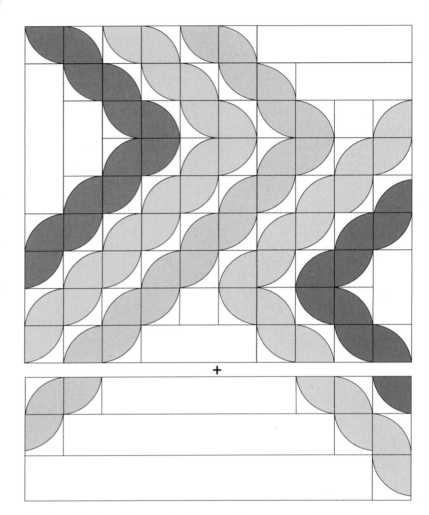

1. Sew **Section Two** to the bottom of **Section One**. Press seam down. See the assembling diagram.

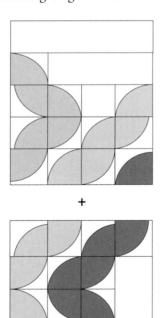

2. Sew **Section Four** to the bottom of **Section Three**. Press seam up. Sew the two halves together and press seam to one side.

3. Sew **Section Five** to the bottom. Press seams. Quilt and bind.

Focal Point Quilt

Does this pattern remind you a bit of "googly eyes"? I love how it draws the eye to the center of the quilt, but depending on where you want your focus, you could turn the circles to all face that spot. It's pretty cool. Inset circles bring a special kind of satisfaction when completed correctly, and this quilt pattern will give you lots of practice. By the end, you'll be a pro!

Before You Start

Read through all the directions and steps before you start. All seams are sewn with a ¼" seam allowance. **All templates need to be printed at 100%** and *not* "fit to page." You can adjust this in your printer settings. Verify that your template is printed at the correct size by measuring all sides of the 1" reference square. If you do not want to print templates, you can use the "Circle Savvy Ruler" by Creative Grids®.

For more inspiration, check out the hashtag #focalpointquilt and #kileysquiltroom. Be sure to use these when you post pictures of your quilt to share with others!

WOF = Width of Fabric
RST = Right Sides Together

Supplies

Templates (pages 112–116)

FABRIC REQUIREMENTS

	Baby 48" x 48"	Small Throw 60" x 60"	Large Throw 72" x 72"	Twin 72" x 96"
Color 1	1 yard	1¾ yard	2¼ yards	3 yards
Color 2	2 yards	3 yards	3¾ yards	5 yards
Color 3	2¼ yards	3½ yards	4¼ yards	6 yards
Background	2½ yards	3½ yards	4¾ yards	6¼ yards
Backing	3 yards	3¾ yards	4½ yards	6½ yards
Binding	½ yard	½ yard	¾ yard	¾ yard

CUTTING INSTRUCTIONS

	Baby 16 blocks	Small Throw 25 blocks	Large Throw 36 blocks	Twin 48 blocks
Color 1	(4) 8½" x WOF, subcut: (16) 8½" x 8½"	(5) 8½" x WOF, subcut: (25) 8½" x 8½"	(9) 8½" x WOF, subcut: (36) 8½" x 8½"	(12) 8½" x WOF, subcut: (48) 8½" x 8½"
Color 2	(6) 11" x WOF, subcut: (16) 11" x 11"	(9) 12" x WOF, subcut: (25) 12" x 12"	(12) 11" x WOF, subcut: (36) 11" x 11"	(16) 11" x WOF, subcut: (48) 11" x 11"
Color 3	(6) 13" x WOF, subcut: (16) 13" x 13"	(9) 14" x WOF, subcut: (25) 14" x 14"	(12) 13" x WOF, subcut: (36) 13" x 13"	(16) 13" x WOF, subcut: (48) 13" x 13"
Background	(6) 13½" x WOF, subcut: (16) 13½" x 13½"	(9) 13½" x WOF, subcut: (25) 13½" x 13½"	(12) 13½" x WOF, subcut: (36) 13½" x 13½"	(16) 13½" x WOF, subcut: (48) 13½" x 13½"

Prepping the Blocks

1. Fold all the color squares in half once and press folded edge. Fold all the Color 1 pieces a second time in half in the other direction and press the folded edge. This will give you crease marks to center your templates.

2. Center the *Circle #1 Inner Template* on each Color 1 square. Cut around the template. Make a mark ½" up from the bottom of the Color 2 squares, centered. Place the bottom edge of the *Circle #1 Background Template* on the ½" mark, and center from both sides. Cut around the template. Repeat with the

Color 3 squares with the *Circle #2 Background Template*, and the background squares with the *Circle #3 Background Template*.

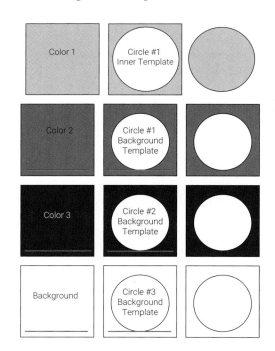

Assembling the Blocks

1. Fold the Color 1 piece and the Color 2 piece in half three times. Press folds to create creases. Lay the Color 2 frame on top of the Color 1 circle. Use the second half of the inset-circle method (page 38) to create the inset-circle block.

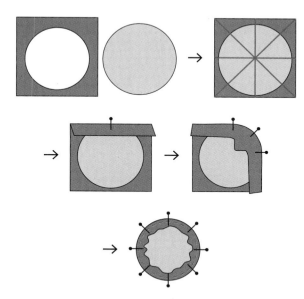

2. Place the *Circle #2 Inner Template* on top of the inset-circle block. The template should rest where you drew a line, ¼" from the bottom. Cut around the template.

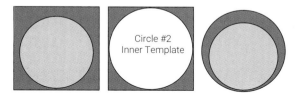

3. Use the inset-circle method to sew the inset-circle pieces into the Color 3 frame.

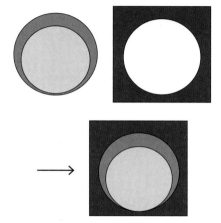

4. Place the *Circle #3 Inner Template* on top of the inset-circle block. The template should rest where you drew a line. Cut around the template.

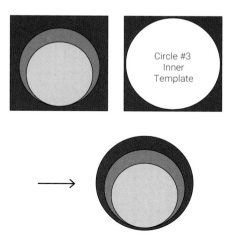

5. Fold your inset circle in half and in half again. Press to crease. Draw or make a crease from corner to corner on the background pieces. Line up the creases on the two pieces and follow the inset-circle method to sew the inset-circle pieces into the background frame. Trim all squares to 12½" x 12½", making sure to leave a ¼" seam allowance on all sides.

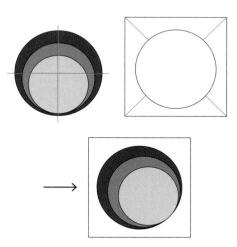

Assembling the Quilt Top

1. Arrange the blocks how you want according to which size quilt you are making.

2. Sew rows together and press each row in one direction, making sure that each row is pressed in the opposite direction from the row before it so that the seams will nest. Sew the rows to one another and press all seams down. Quilt and bind.

☐ Twin ☐ Large Throw ☐ Small Throw ☐ Baby

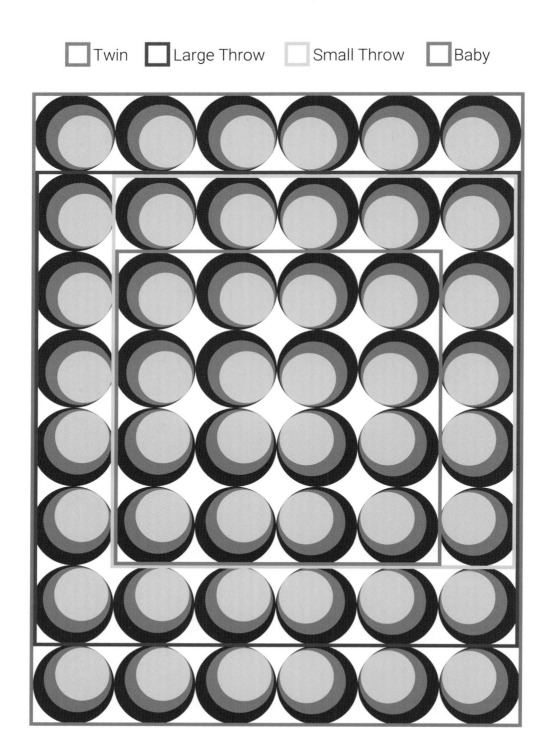

Starry-Eyed Quilt

I love a pattern that combines skills! It keeps me on my toes and makes a pattern more fun! This pattern has HSTs and curves in it to help practice the skills you have learned.

Before You Start

Read through all the directions and steps before you start. All seams are sewn with a ¼" seam allowance. **All templates need to be printed at 100%** and *not* "fit to page." You can adjust this in your printer settings. Verify that your template is printed at the correct size by measuring all sides of the 1" reference square.

For more inspiration, check out the hashtag #starryeyedquilt and #kileysquiltroom. Be sure to use these when you post pictures of your quilt to share with others!

WOF = Width of Fabric
RST = Right Sides Together

Supplies

Templates (page 123)

FABRIC REQUIREMENTS

	Throw 56" x 56"	Twin 70" x 98"	Queen 84" x 98"	King 112" x 98"
Dark Color	1 yard	2 yards	2¼ yard	3 yards
Light Color	1 yard	2 yards	2¼ yards	3 yards
Dark Accent	¼ yard	¾ yard	1 yard	1¼ yards
Medium Accent	½ yard	½ yard	¾ yard	1 yard
Light Accent	¼ yard	½ yard	¾ yard	1 yard
Background	2¾ yards	5¾ yards	6¾ yards	9 yards
Backing	3½ yards	6½ yards	7¾ yards	10 yards
Binding	½ yard	¾ yard	¾ yard	1 yard

CUTTING INSTRUCTIONS

	Throw 16 blocks	Twin 35 blocks	Queen 42 blocks	King 56 blocks
Background	(11) 4½" x WOF, subcut: (128) 4½" x 3½" (8) 5" x WOF, subcut: (64) 5" x 5"	(24) 4½" x WOF, subcut: (280) 4½" x 3½" (18) 5" x WOF, subcut: (140) 5" x 5"	(28) 4½" x WOF, subcut: (336) 4½" x 3½" (21) 5" x WOF, subcut: (168) 5" x 5"	(38) 4½" x WOF, subcut: (448) 4½" x 3½" (29) 5" x WOF, subcut: (232) 5" x 5"
Dark Color	(1) 14" x WOF, subcut: (2) 14" x 14" (16) 3½" x 3½" (4) 3½" x WOF, subcut: (48) 3½" x 3½"	(2) 14" x WOF, subcut: (5) 14" x 14" (16) 3½" x 3½" (11) 3½" x WOF, subcut: (124) 3½" x 3½"	(2) 14" x WOF, subcut: (5) 14" x 14" (16) 3½" x 3½" (13) 3½" x WOF, subcut: (152) 3½" x 3½"	(3) 14" x WOF, subcut: (7) 14" x 14" (32) 3½" x 3½" (16) 3½" x WOF, subcut: (192) 3½" x 3½"
Light Color	(1) 14" x WOF, subcut: (2) 14" x 14" (16) 3½" x 3½" (4) 3½" x WOF, subcut: (48) 3½" x 3½"	(2) 14" x WOF, subcut: (5) 14" x 14" (16) 3½" x 3½" (11) 3½" x WOF, subcut: (124) 3½" x 3½"	(2) 14" x WOF, subcut: (5) 14" x 14" (16) 3½" x 3½" (13) 3½" x WOF, subcut: (152) 3½" x 3½"	(3) 14" x WOF, subcut: (7) 14" x 14" (32) 3½" x 3½" (16) 3½" x WOF, subcut: (192) 3½" x 3½"
Dark Accent	(2) 4" x WOF, subcut: (16) 4" x 4"	(6) 4" x WOF, subcut: (60) 4" x 4"	(8) 4" x WOF, subcut: (72) 4" x 4"	(10) 4" x WOF, subcut: (96) 4" x 4"
Medium Accent	(4) 4" x WOF, subcut: (32) 4" x 4"	(4) 4" x WOF, subcut: (40) 4" x 4"	(5) 4" x WOF, subcut: (48) 4" x 4"	(7) 4" x WOF, subcut: (64) 4" x 4"
Light Accent	(2) 4" x WOF, subcut: (16) 4" x 4"	(4) 4" x WOF, subcut: (40) 4" x 4"	(5) 4" x WOF, subcut: (48) 4" x 4"	(7) 4" x WOF, subcut: (64) 4" x 4"

Curves

1. Place *Template A* on all Accent Color squares and cut along the curve. Keep the quarter-circle piece. Place *Template B* on all 5" x 5" background squares and cut along the curve. Keep the frame piece.

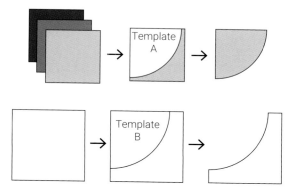

2. Sew the two curved pieces together using the quarter-circle method (page 38). Press seams toward the accent color. Trim all the blocks to 4½" x 4½".

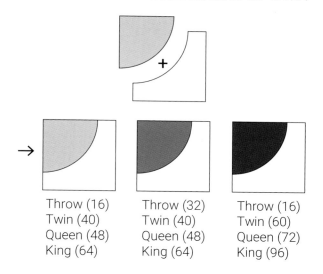

Throw (16)
Twin (40)
Queen (48)
King (64)

Throw (32)
Twin (40)
Queen (48)
King (64)

Throw (16)
Twin (60)
Queen (72)
King (96)

HSTs

1. Place the 14" x 14" Dark Color and Light Color squares RST. Make HSTs using the eight-at-a-time method (page 11). Press seams to the darker side. Trim all HSTs to 6½" x 6½".

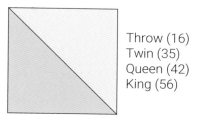

Throw (16)
Twin (35)
Queen (42)
King (56)

2. Draw a diagonal line on the backs of all 3½" x 3½" Dark Color and Light Color squares. Place them, RST, on one end of the 4½" x 3½" background pieces. Half of the diagonal lines should come to the bottom-right corner and half to the bottom-left corner, as shown. Sew on the diagonal. Press seams to the darker side. Trim the excess off, leaving a ¼" seam allowance. Sew these blocks together in mirroring pairs, as shown. Press seams.

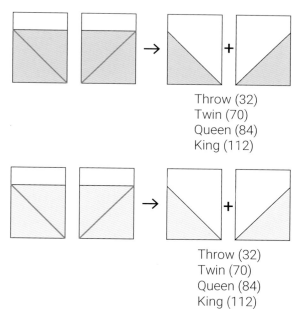

Throw (32)
Twin (70)
Queen (84)
King (112)

Throw (32)
Twin (70)
Queen (84)
King (112)

Assembling the Blocks

1. Sew (1) mirroring set to the sides of the 6½" x 6½" HSTs. Make sure that the correct colors are touching. Press seams in toward the center.

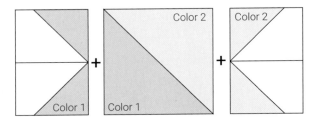

2. Following the diagram, sew together rows using the mirrored sets and the Accent-Color curved blocks. Press seams away from the center of the row.

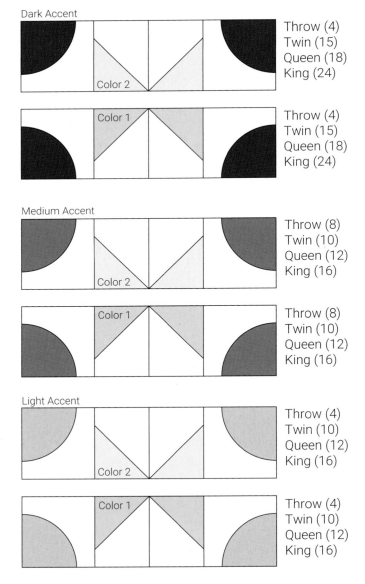

Dark Accent

Throw (4)
Twin (15)
Queen (18)
King (24)

Throw (4)
Twin (15)
Queen (18)
King (24)

Medium Accent

Throw (8)
Twin (10)
Queen (12)
King (16)

Throw (8)
Twin (10)
Queen (12)
King (16)

Light Accent

Throw (4)
Twin (10)
Queen (12)
King (16)

Throw (4)
Twin (10)
Queen (12)
King (16)

3. Following the diagram, sew the rows together into blocks, nesting seams as you go. Press seams.

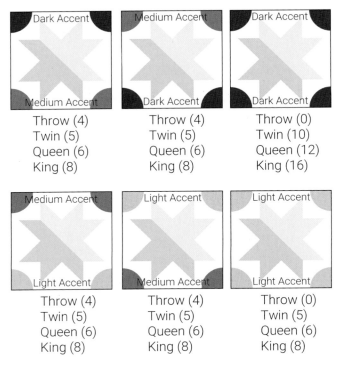

Dark Accent / Medium Accent	Medium Accent / Dark Accent	Dark Accent / Dark Accent
Throw (4)	Throw (4)	Throw (0)
Twin (5)	Twin (5)	Twin (10)
Queen (6)	Queen (6)	Queen (12)
King (8)	King (8)	King (16)

Medium Accent / Light Accent	Light Accent / Medium Accent	Light Accent / Light Accent
Throw (4)	Throw (4)	Throw (0)
Twin (5)	Twin (5)	Twin (5)
Queen (6)	Queen (6)	Queen (6)
King (8)	King (8)	King (8)

Assembling the Quilt Top

1. Following the diagram, assemble your Throw-Size Quilt Top. Bed-Size Quilt Top assembly is on page 67. Sew blocks into rows first, pressing seams in each row in one direction and the next row in the opposite direction. Sew the rows to each other, following the order shown. Press seams. Quilt and bind.

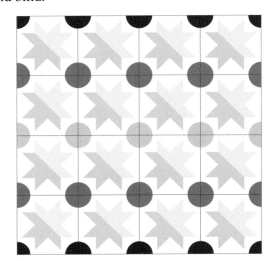

2. Following the diagram, assemble your Bed-Size Quilt Top. Sew blocks into rows first, pressing seams in each row in one direction and the next row in the opposite direction. Sew the rows to each other, following the order shown. Press seams. Quilt and bind.

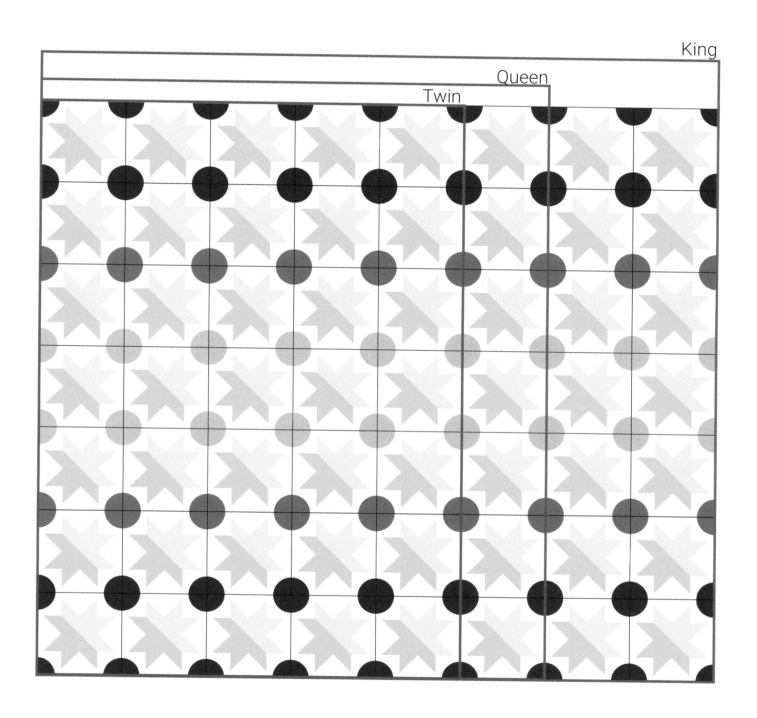

Intro to Appliqué

There are lots of different ways to do **appliqué**! Appliqué is the process of applying fabric and shapes onto your quilt top. The two main techniques are raw edge and needle turn.

Raw-Edge Appliqué

Raw-edge appliqué is cutting out your shapes and stitching them down—often leaving a raw edge that can fray—which is fine if you want that added dimension of texture on your quilt. You can stitch your shapes down just inside the shape or further in, depending on how much fray you want to have. You can also use a blanket stitch (either by hand or on a machine that has that option) around the edges to tack down your shapes and hide the fraying.

Needle-Turn Appliqué

Needle-turn appliqué has a much cleaner edge but takes a lot more effort to achieve. It is where you turn under the edges of your appliqué shapes and use tiny (almost invisible) whip stitches to tack down the edges.

Holding Down Appliqué

Both techniques use a variety of ways to hold your appliqué pieces in place while you stitch them down. The most common is either pins or a double-sided fusible paper. This fuses your pieces down so you don't have to hold them in place, and it keeps their shape so they don't move or warp while you sew.

Mod Quilter's Baseball Cap

Are you a soccer mom? Or maybe you know someone who is? I have four kids who are all in different sports and activities. Sometimes I don't always get the chance to shower before we have to run out the door. Grabbing a cute baseball cap is my way of leveling up on days when I just don't have the time or energy!

Before You Start

Read through all the directions and steps before you start.

For more inspiration, check out the hashtag #modquilterscap and #kileysquiltroom. Be sure to use these when you post pictures of your quilt to share with others!

> **Supplies**
>
> Templates (page 155)
> Baseball cap
> Fabric scraps
> Double-sided fusible paper (I used HeatnBond)

Appliqué

1. Draw or trace whatever shapes you want on double-sided HeatnBond.

2. Iron one side of the HeatnBond to your fabric. For the star design, I first sewed two scraps together and then aligned the star diagonally on the seam before adhering.

3. Cut the fabric out along the drawn lines.

4. Peel off the second side of the HeatnBond. Iron the shape to the baseball hat.

5. Stitch around the shape. You can do a blanket stitch, straight stitch, zigzag stitch, or whatever you choose!

6. For the leaf design, I first applied the light green shape. Then repeat the steps again with each dark green shape, overlapping for a fun effect.

TIP

Be sure to check the fabric of your hat. If it is synthetic, you'll want to turn the heat on your iron down to prevent melting your hat.

Boho Art Wall Hangings
Makes three 18" x 40" panels

Appliqué opens unlimited creative possibilities in your textile art. In this project, I created three wall hanging panels that complement each other and are the perfect way to show off your artistic abilities in your home.

This design requires layering your appliqué pieces. You can stitch down one layer at a time, or you can secure them all and then stitch them down. Either way, it is a stunning piece!

Before You Start

Read through all the directions and steps before you start. **All templates need to be printed at 100%** and *not* "fit to page." You can adjust this in your printer settings. Verify that your template is printed at the correct size by measuring all sides of the 1" reference square. You may notice that all the templates are printed as a mirror image of what they look like in the diagrams. Don't worry, they are correct when you finish.

For more inspiration, check out the hashtag #bohoartwallquilts and #kileysquiltroom. Be sure to use these when you post pictures of your quilt to share with others!

FABRIC REQUIREMENTS

	All 3 Panels 18" x 40" each
Colors 1–5	1 Fat Quarter each
Background	1½ yards
Backing	2 yards
Binding	¾ yard

Supplies

Templates (pages 124–128)
Double-sided fusible paper (I used HeatnBond)

TRACING TEMPLATES

#	Amount
1	6
2	6
3	6
4	23
5	2
6	4
7	2
8	2
9	3
10	9
11	7
12	9

Appliqué

1. Print the templates and then trace them onto HeatnBond. Make sure you have the right number of each shape (see chart). Cut each shape out close to the lines but not on the lines. Label your pieces as you go.

2. Arrange your pieces on the Fat Quarters as shown. Iron each fusible piece to the **back** of your fabric pieces and cut them out on the lines.

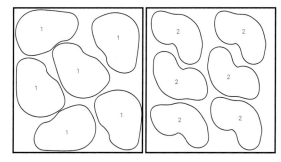

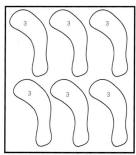

3. Place your pieces on the panels in layers as shown in the diagrams on the next couple of sections.

Panel 1

1. Place your first layer down and arrange as desired or as close to the diagram as possible. Iron in place.

2. Lay down the next layer and iron in place.

3. Go around each piece with a zigzag stitch, blanket stitch, or embroidering stitch. Use coordinating threads for best coordination. Quilt and bind to complete.

Panel 2

1. Place your first layer down and arrange as desired or as close to the diagram as possible. Iron in place.

2. Lay down the next layer and iron in place.

3. Go around each piece with a zigzag stitch, blanket stitch, or embroidering stitch. Use coordinating threads for best coordination. Quilt and bind to complete.

Panel 3

1. Place your first layer down and arrange as desired or as close to the diagram as possible. Iron in place.

2. Lay down the next layer and iron in place.

3. Go around each piece with a zigzag stitch, blanket stitch, or embroidering stitch. Use coordinating threads for best coordination. Quilt and bind to complete.

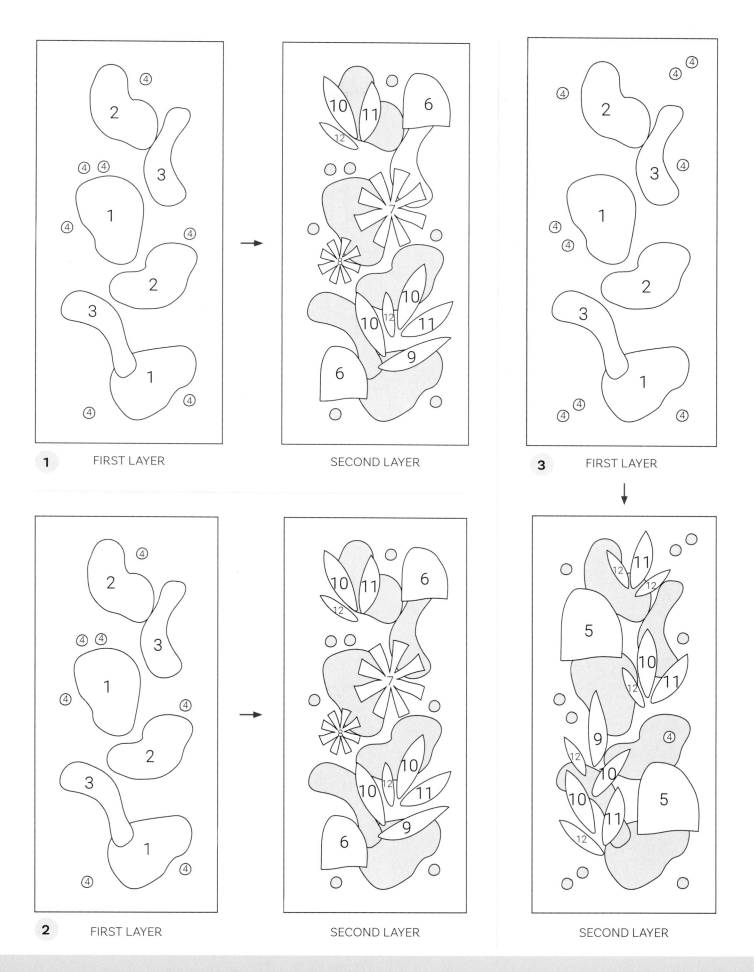

1   FIRST LAYER

SECOND LAYER

3   FIRST LAYER

2   FIRST LAYER

SECOND LAYER

SECOND LAYER

Intro to Improv

Improv is exactly what it sounds like. It's letting your own creativity guide you as you quilt. This is a great way to use up scraps or extra blocks. There are many techniques for various improv styles. But always make sure that the two edges you are about to sew together match up! If they are two straight edges, they both need to be exactly straight; if they are curved, the curves need to match up exactly. Doing this will help you get nice, flat results.

Here are some ideas for piecing your next improv project:

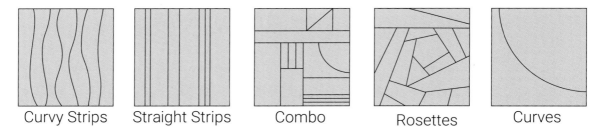

Curvy Strips   Straight Strips   Combo   Rosettes   Curves

It is difficult to write an improv pattern since the very definition is supposed to be spontaneous. The following patterns will give you a general idea of what your outcome *could* look like. But it is totally up to you. Play with it! Let your imagination run wild and see what your creation becomes.

We will start small with some scraps and small clothes patches and work our way up to a whole quilt.

Improv Clothes Patch

Quilted clothing or accents on clothing has been a rising fashion trend! But why pay for accents when you can get exactly what you want yourself?

Square Patch

This first option is going to be patches on your jeans, but you don't need a hole to add this cute detail.

1. Create (2) 4½" x 4½" improv blocks. Use the options on page 76 for inspiration, create from your own imagination, or repurpose an extra quilt block from your fabric stash.

2. If you wish to make the blocks look quilted, cut (2) 4" x 4" pieces of thin batting. Quilt one to the back of each patch. I know it will feel weird that the batting is smaller, but it will help you! Fold ¼" of the fabric to the back around all the edges. Press.

3. Apply (1) 4" x 4" square of HeatnBond to the backs of the patches, and iron in place on your jeans. I like to overlap my two patches on one pant leg, but feel free to do what feels right for you. Either hand stitch or machine stitch the patches down.

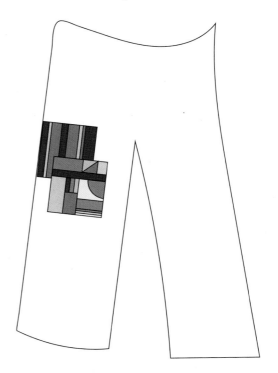

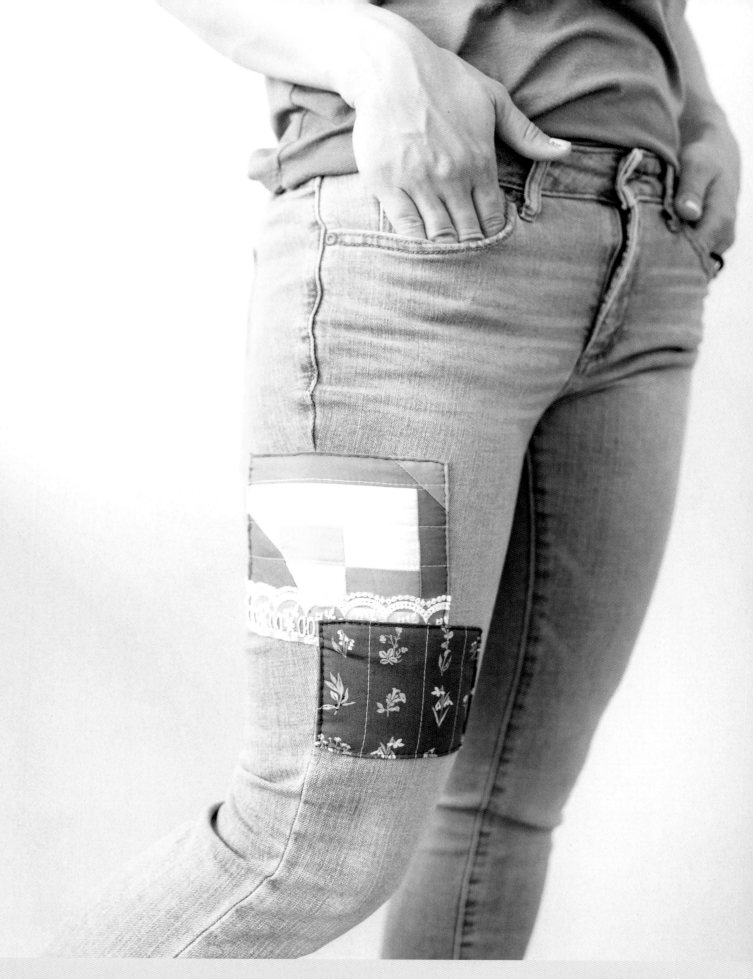

Specific-Area Patch

The second method is a little more precise. We are going to match the patches to a specific area of clothing.

1. Using some paper, trace a back pocket on your jeans, a hooded-sweatshirt pocket, or a hooded-sweatshirt hood. Add ½" all the way around the shape you traced and cut it out. Create an improv block that is bigger than the shape you cut out. Once you are done creating your improv block, place your paper shape on top and cut out your shape.

2. If you wish to make the patch look quilted, cut a piece of thin batting that is ½" smaller than your shape on all edges. Quilt it to the back of your patch. Turn all the edges to the back and press.

3. Pin your patch in place, lining up all the edges with the edges of the shape on your clothes. Sew in place. If you are sewing it to a pocket, ensure you do not sew the pocket closed. You can sew all the edges down first and then hand sew the edges of the pocket openings so that it can still be used.

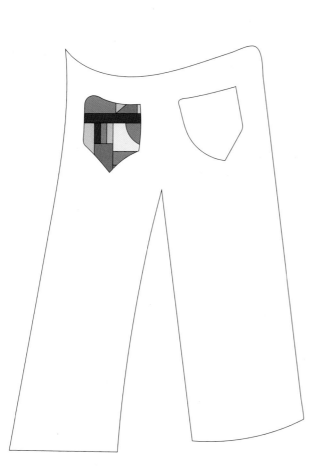 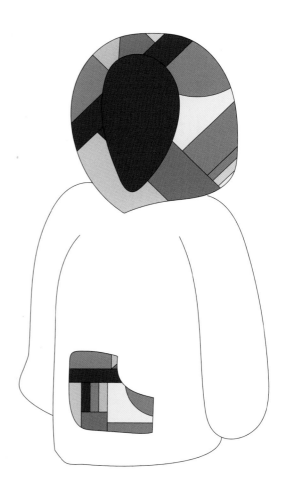

Flow Quilt

Let's try some improv on a large scale! Keep in mind that this is just a general walk through of how to complete a **similar** quilt. Since it is improv, yours will and should look a bit different!

Before You Start

Read through all the directions and steps before you start. All seams are sewn with a ¼" seam allowance.

For more inspiration, check out the hashtag #flowquilt and #kileysquiltroom. Be sure to use these when you post pictures of your quilt to share with others!

WOF = Width of Fabric
RST = Right Sides Together

FABRIC REQUIREMENTS

	Small Throw 42" x 50"
Colors 1–3	¾ yard each
Color 4	½ yard
Backing	2½ yards
Binding	⅓ yard

CUTTING INSTRUCTIONS

	Small Throw 42" x 50"
Colors 1–3	(2) 12" x WOF, subcut: (2) 12" x 40½" of each color
Color 4	(1) 12" x WOF, subcut: (1) 12" x 40½"

Assembling the Quilt Top

1. Take (1) strip of Color 1 and draw a wavy line along one of the long edges. Make sure that your line does not exceed 3". Cut along this wavy line.

2. Place (1) strip of Color 2 underneath the Color 1 piece. Make sure that Color 1 overlaps the top edge of the Color 2 strip by ½" at the highest point of the Color 1's wavy line. Trace the wavy line onto the Color 2 strip.

3. Mark perpendicular lines every 5" or so along the wavy line. Make sure the marks are drawn across both fabrics. Remove the Color 1 strip. Cut along the wavy line of the Color 2 strip.

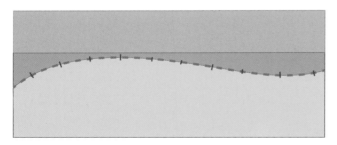

4. Pin the fabrics together where you made the perpendicular marks. It will feel "wrong," but trust the process! Also, your ends may not match up exactly; be sure to account for your seam allowance. Sew your pieces together, careful to keep the edges together all along the way. Press the seam toward Color 2.

5. Repeat this process, following the Quilt Layout Guide, until you get to the last strip.

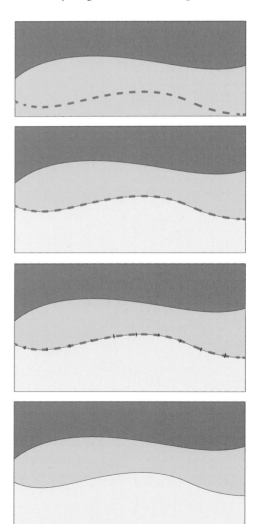

Quilt Layout Guide

1. Use this layout guide to order your strips when recreating this look. Your wavy lines will look much different than mine!

2. Once you are done sewing the rows together, square up the quilt. Quilt and bind.

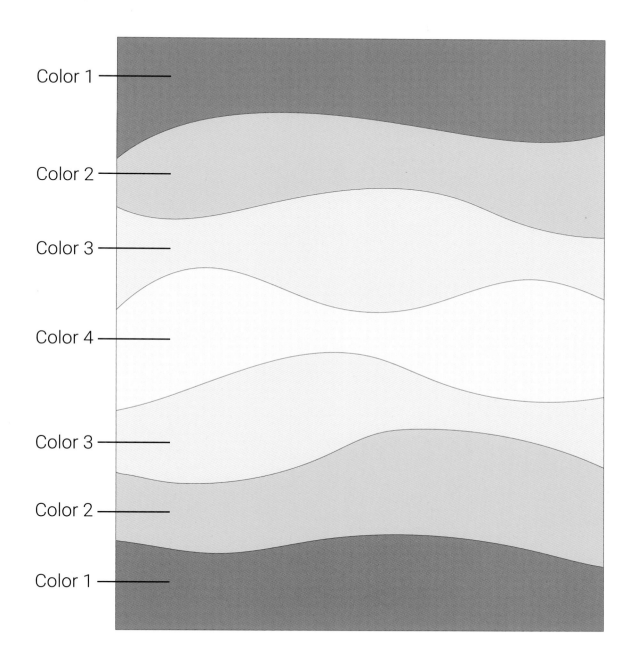

Color 1

Color 2

Color 3

Color 4

Color 3

Color 2

Color 1

Intro to FPP

Foundation Paper Piecing (FPP) is the technique of using lines on paper as the template for your block. This technique allows you to create angles and shapes that would be very difficult to achieve with traditional piecing methods. FPP patterns can range from very simple to extremely complex.

There are two very important things to know about FPP. The first is that paper matters! You are sewing fabric directly to the paper. Thus, you need something that is durable enough to print on but thin enough to tear off when you are done. You can use a very lightweight printer paper, or you can purchase FPP paper from craft stores and online. Either works great!

The second most important thing to know about FPP is that, however your block looks on paper, your fabric block will be the reverse image. You are sewing your fabrics to the back of the paper, so the resulting block is in reverse.

Most FPP patterns or blocks are numbered. You will just follow the number order when attaching fabric. I like to start by using a dab of washable glue on the first section to hold the fabric in place until sewing on the next piece. When you are all done adding pieces, trim your block. It is a very simple concept once you get the hang of it!

Example

Let's take a look at the Deviate quilt pattern (Deviate quilt pattern can be found on my website: kileysquiltroom.com).

The block is broken into two sections. Start on the back of the block that has Section 1. Glue a piece of fabric to the paper labeled Section 1, ensuring the fabric covers the whole section. Trim ¼" away from the line to Section 2. Line up the next piece under piece one, along the trimmed edge. Sew on the line. Continue with each section until the block is finished! As you can see, it is a mirror image to the paper template.

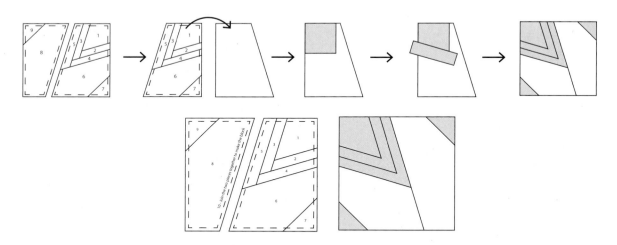

FPP Star Clock

I love to decorate my sewing space with my work! This clock pattern is a great way to add some quilting flare to your walls without being too heavy or overwhelming! This pattern combines FPP and curved piecing!

Before You Start

Read through all the directions and steps before you start. **All templates need to be printed at 100%** and *not* "fit to page." You can adjust this in your printer settings. Verify that your template is printed at the correct size by measuring all sides of the 1" reference square.

For more inspiration, check out the hashtag #FPPStarClock and #kileysquiltroom. Be sure to use these when you post pictures of your project to share with others!

FPP = Foundation Paper Piecing
RST = Right Sides Together

Supplies

Templates (pages 129–130)
(1) FQ each of light and dark fabric
¾ yard background fabric; cut (1) 20" x 20" square and use the rest for FPP
20" x ¼" elastic
(1) 13" wood round; drill a hole into the center for the clock mechanism
(1) clock motor and arms
Disappearing fabric pen

TIP

If you'd like to buy a hardware kit for this clock (includes the wood with a drilled hole in the center, clock motor, clock hands, and elastic), go to my website: www.kileysquiltroom.com

FPP

1. Following the FPP instructions (page 86), sew all your sections. You should have (12) total sections. I made half in a light blue and half in a dark blue.

2. Sew (6) sections together, and repeat, to make (2) half circles. Make sure to alternate the colors. When sewing the wedges together, do not go all the way to the point. Stop about ⅛" away from the point, and backstitch to stabilize the point. Press the seams all up on one half circle and all down the other half circle.

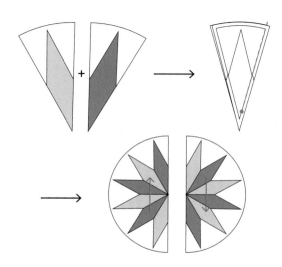

3. Sew the two sections together, RST. Sew toward the middle, but stop ¼" away from the center; backstitch to stabilize. Repeat on the other side. Press this seam open.

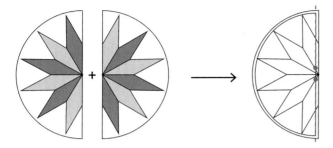

4. Fold the 20" background fabric piece into quarters as precisely as possible. Line up the *Inset-Circle Template* with the corner of the two folded edges. Cut along the curve. Use the "frame" piece and not the inner-circle piece.

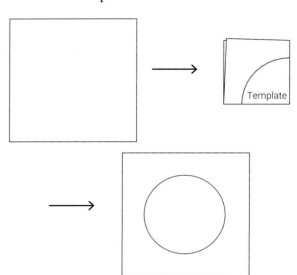

5. Following the inset-circle method (page 38), sew the background frame around the FPP-constructed center circle. Press the seam away from the center. Fold the block in half and in half again. Measure 3⅝" away from the curved seam, marking with a fabric pen 5–6 times along the curve. Draw a curved line to connect your marks and cut along the curved line. It does not need to be perfect. You will not see this cut from the front of the clock.

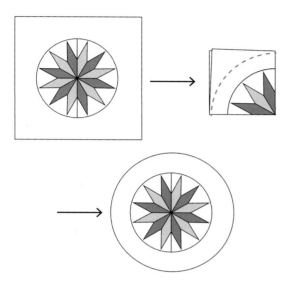

6. Carefully press ½" of the edge of the circle to the back. It's okay if it has puckers or folds. Stitch the fold down ⅛" away from the raw edge all the way around the circle, leaving a 1" gap.

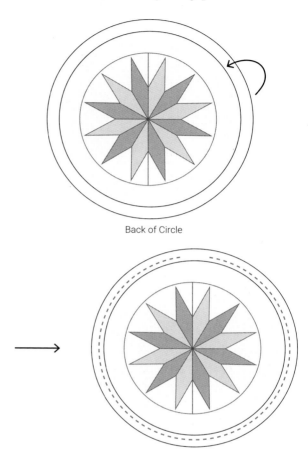

Back of Circle

7. Insert a safety pin into each end of the elastic string. Put one end into the sleeve and work it all the way around the circle until it comes out through the gap. Make sure to not lose the other end in the sleeve as well. Overlap the ends and sew together. Sew the gap closed.

8. Fit the clock cover over the wood circle. Assemble the clock components according to the instructions. The center star points were not sewn all the way to allow the clock arms and motor to be inserted. Make sure that the FPP star has a point facing directly up and down before hanging it on the wall so that you can tell time with it.

Jack-O-Quilt

Every Halloween, my husband and I carve pumpkins with our kids, and it's always so fun to make a new face on each pumpkin. We love to line them up on the porch and put little lights in them so the faces will glow. A favorite holiday activity for many families, I'm sure. This design is the quilted embodiment of this tradition. You could even use glowing fabric or thread on the faces to give an seven spookier element for your holiday!

Foundation Paper Piecing may seem daunting because it focuses on precision piecing. But since you are sewing directly to the paper and on the lines, it's hard to get it wrong once you have a feel for the process. One of the nice things about FPP patterns, in general, is there are no real cutting instructions (unless, like this one, it has borders). You just snip pieces off as you go!

Before You Start

Read through all the directions and steps before you start. **All templates need to be printed at 100%** and *not* "fit to page." You can adjust this in your printer settings. Verify that your template is printed at the correct size by measuring all sides of the 1" reference square. I suggest using a very thin paper.

FPP patterns are tricky to get exact fabric requirements for. These provided are rough estimates. You may want to get a bit extra just in case. The cutting instructions for the background are just for the borders that you will add to the blocks and quilt top.

FPP = Foundation Paper Piecing

Supplies

Templates (pages 131–152)
Add-A-Quarter ruler

FABRIC REQUIREMENTS & CUTTING

	Small Throw 42" x 42"
Jack-o'-Lantern Faces	¾ yard
Background (FPP)	2 yards
Backing	3 yards
Binding	½ yard
Background (Sashing and Borders)	(11) 1½" x WOF, subcut: (18) 1½" x 10½" (18) 1½" x 12½" (4) 3½" x WOF, subcut: (2) 3½" x 36½" (2) 3½" x 42½"

1. Cut out your templates and organize them into nine piles according to the jack-o'-lantern faces. Each template will say which face it belongs to. Following the FPP instructions (page 86), add your fabric one piece at a time in order, using the numbered sections on the templates. When measuring a section to cut a piece of fabric, lay the template down over the fabric and cut a piece that is at least ¼" larger on all sides than the section it will go on.

2. Follow the piecing instructions for each block to put the templates together. See the diagrams as an example:

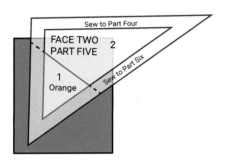

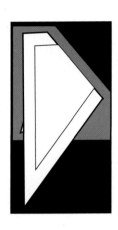

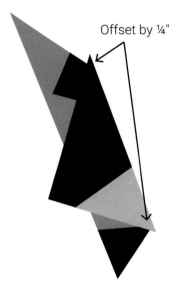

Offset by ¼"

Glue this first piece to the back of your template, making sure that the edges of your fabric cover all edges of this section.

Fold along the line you will sew on next. Cut ¼" away from the edge, as shown in orange. Place a piece of fabric underneath that covers the next section while folded over, as shown in black.

Be sure to sew your lines all the way to the edge of the template. Also, offset your sections when lining them up to sew them together, as shown. The smaller/narrower angle is the one that should hang over the other section.

Face One

1. Sew Parts 3 and 4 together and press the seam to one side. Add Part 2 and press. Add Part 5 and press. Sew together Part 1 and Parts 2–5 to get the top half of the face.

2. Sew Parts 6–11 together as shown, pressing all seams to one side. This is the bottom half of the face. Sew it to the bottom of the top half and press seam. This is **Face One**.

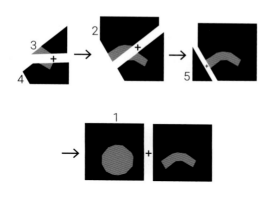

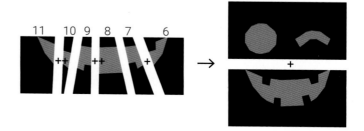

Face Two

1. Sew Parts 7, 6, and 5 together as shown, pressing seams to one side. Sew together Parts 2 and 3. To create the left half of the face, sew Part 4 to the top of Parts 5–6.

2. To create the right half of the face, sew Part 1 to the top of Parts 2–3. Press seams. Sew the two halves together to make **Face Two**.

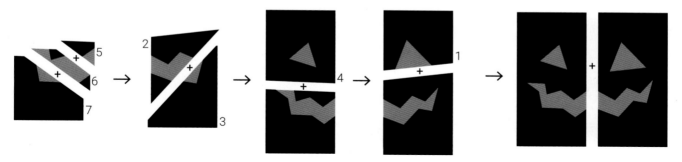

Face Three

1. Sew Parts 1 and 2 together and press seam. Add Part 3 and press. Add Part 4 and press. Add Part 5 and press. This is **Face Three**.

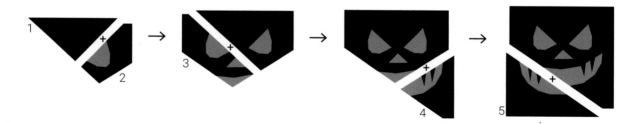

Face Four

1. Sew Parts 1 and 2 together and press seam to one side. Add Part 3 to the bottom and press. This is the top half of the face. Sew Parts 5–7 together as shown, pressing seams to one side. Add part 4 and press. This is the bottom half of the face.

2. Sew the top half and the bottom half of the face together. Press to one side. This is **Face Four**.

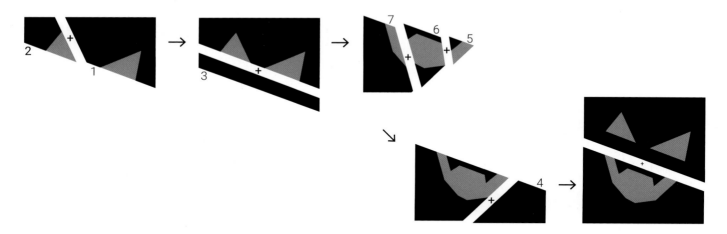

Face Five

1. Sew Parts 1 and 2 together and press to one side. Sew together Parts 5–8 as shown, and press all seams to one side. Sew this section to the Parts 1–2 section. Press seams. This is the top half of the face.

2. Sew Parts 3 and 4 together and press seams. This is the bottom half of the face. Sew the two halves together and press seams. This is **Face Five**.

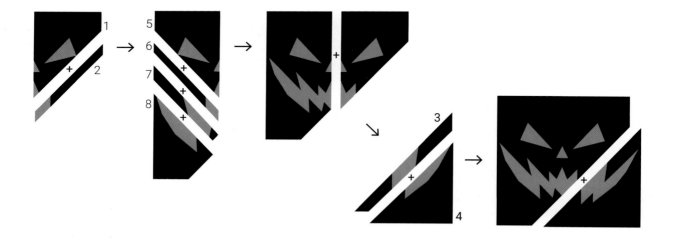

Face Six

1. Sew Parts 3 and 4 together and press seams. Add Part 1 to the top and press. This is the left half of the face.

2. Sew Parts 5 and 6 together and press seams. Sew Part 4 to the top of the 5–6 section, then sew Part 7 to the bottom. Press seams to one side. This is the right half of the face. Sew the two halves together and press. This is **Face Six**.

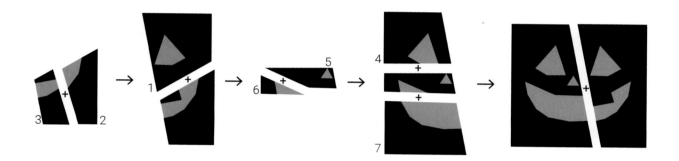

Face Seven

1. Sew Parts 1 and 2 together and press to one side. This is the top half of the face. Sew Parts 3–7 together and press all seams to one side. This is the bottom half of the face. Sew the two halves together and press the seam. This is **Face Seven**.

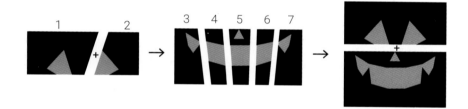

Face Eight

1. Sew Part 2 to Part 3 and press. Add Part 1 and press the seam. Add Part 4 and press. This is **Face Eight**.

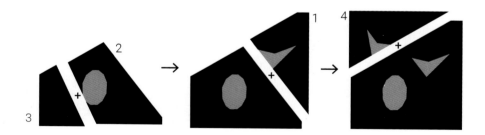

Face Nine

1. Sew Parts 2–4 together and press seams to one side. Add Part 1 as shown and press seam. This is the top half of the face.

2. Sew Parts 5–7 together and press seams to one side. Add Part 8 as shown and press seam. This is the bottom half of the face. Sew the two halves together and press. This is **Face Nine**.

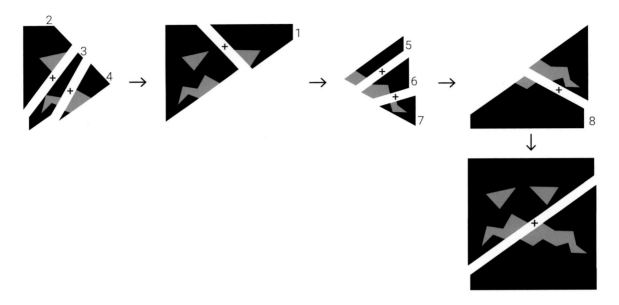

Sashing

1. Sew (2) 1½" x 10½" background strips to the top and bottom of each face block. Press seams out toward the sashing. Sew (2) 1½" x 12½" strips to the sides of each face block. Press seams out toward the border.

Assembling the Quilt Top

1. Arrange blocks in a 3 x 3 formation. Sew the rows together and press the seams in each row in the opposite direction of the row before it. Sew the rows to each other, nesting seams as you go. Press seams.

2. Sew (2) 3½" x 36½" background strips to the top and bottom of the quilt top. Press seams toward the borders.

3. Sew (2) 3½" x 42½" background strips to the sides. Press seams toward the borders. Quilt and bind.

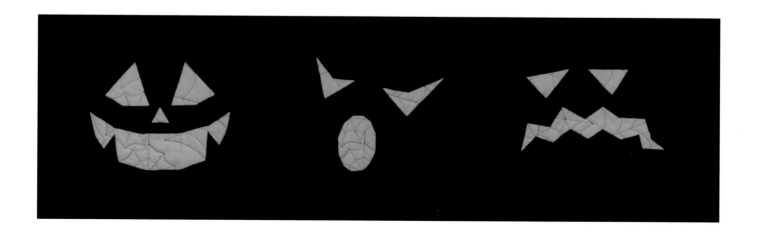

Intro to Y-Seams

I saved this technique for last, probably because I find it the trickiest and the most uncommon in modern quilts. A **Y-seam** is when you have an intersection of three points instead of the typical four. It requires some precision and some forgiveness. Don't give up if you don't get it right away!

Marking Corners

My best tip for getting perfect Y-seams is to mark ¼" away from each corner on the back of every piece. It may seem tedious, but it will really help you with the precision.

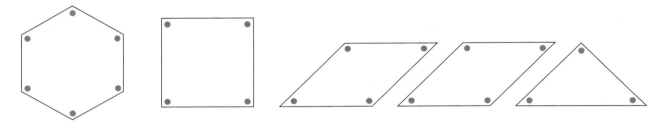

Stabilize Stitch Lines

My second-best tip is to stabilize your stitch lines at the beginning and end of each seam line (where you made your marks). I know this also sounds a bit tedious, but it will help keep your stitches in place since you won't be crossing stitch lines like you normally would in your typical cross seams.

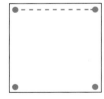

Try it out first with some scraps you don't care about. When you feel confident, move on to your favorite print to make a gorgeous Star or Hexagon pattern.

Storage Bin Slipcovers

Makes one 10½" x 10½" x 11" slipcover

The star design on these slipcovers is a great way to try out Y-seams. Make sure your templates are the right size before you get started to avoid cursing at your work.

Since many storage bin covers are various sizes, you can alter the pattern to fit yours by measuring the front and side panels and cutting your pieces down to the size that you need. For a bonus, you can add a little handle above the star to access your bins more easily.

Before You Start

Read through all the directions and steps before you start. All seams are sewn with a ¼" seam allowance. **All templates need to be printed at 100%** and *not* "fit to page." You can adjust this in your printer settings. Verify that your template is printed at the correct size by measuring all sides of the 1" reference square.

For more inspiration, check out the hashtag #storagebinslipcover and #kileysquiltroom. Be sure to use these when you post pictures of your quilt to share with others!

WOF = Width of Fabric
RST = Right Sides Together
FQ = Fat Quarter

Supplies

Templates (page 153)
10½" x 10½" x 11" bin
(8) 10½" x 12" batting (optional)
(1) 10½" x 10½" batting (optional)
Disappearing fabric pen

FABRIC REQUIREMENTS

Color 1	Color 2	Background
⅛ yard or 1 FQ	⅛ yard or 1 FQ	1½ yards

CUTTING INSTRUCTIONS

Color 1	Color 2	Background
(1) 2½" x WOF, subcut: (4) *Diamond Templates*	(1) 2½" x WOF, subcut: (4) *Diamond Templates*	(1) 3" x WOF, subcut: (4) 3" x 3" (2) 1½" x 12½" (1) 2½" x WOF, subcut: (4) *Triangle Templates* (2) 2¼" x 9" (3) 11" x WOF, subcut: (1) 11" x 11" (7) 11" x 12½"

Prepping the Pieces

1. Gather all the 3" x 3" background pieces, *Triangle Template* background pieces, and *Diamond Template* color pieces. On the backs of these pieces, make a mark with washable ink that is ¼" from each edge on each corner.

Assembling the Pieces

1. Pair up each Color 1 piece with a Color 2 piece. Sew one edge together, starting and stopping at the marks you made at the corners. Backstitch a bit to stabilize the end points. Do not press yet.

2. Sew the background *Triangle Template* pieces between the the two diamond pieces by sewing along one side first, starting and stopping on the marks. Repeat along the next side, starting and stopping on the marks. Do not press yet.

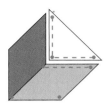

3. Take (2) of these units and sew them together, starting and stopping on the marks. Sew two of these large units together to make a star, as shown. Do not press yet.

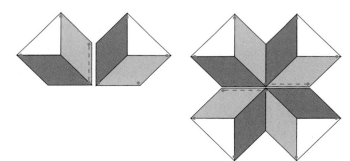

4. Sew (1) 3" x 3" square to each corner of the Star, making sure to start and stop on each marking. Swirl the center seam: arrange all seams that are coming to the center so they are facing the same clockwise or counterclockwise direction. Press. Do this to all seams. The star should measure 9" x 9".

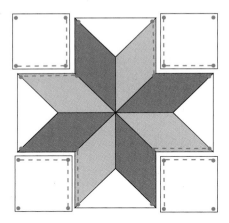

5. Sew (2) 2¼" x 9" background pieces to the top and bottom of the block. Press seams. Sew (2) 1½" x 12½" background pieces to the sides. Press seams. The block should measure 11" x 12½".

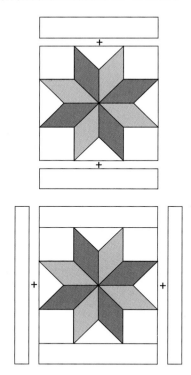

Assembling the Cover

1. Sew the Star block and remaining background pieces together, as shown, by first sewing together the column and then adding the two side "wings." When adding the "wings," center the inner edge with the center square. Stop and start at the seams of the center square. The "wings" should hang past the seams by ¼" on both sides of the center piece. Quilt the constructed pieces to batting if desired.

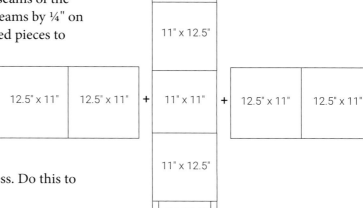

2. With RST, sew two of the "arms" together and press. Do this to all "arms."

3. You should have one long cube with the right sides facing in. If you quilted with batting, bind the open ends of the cube as you would a quilt. If you did not quilt it, roll the raw edges out and top stitch in place.

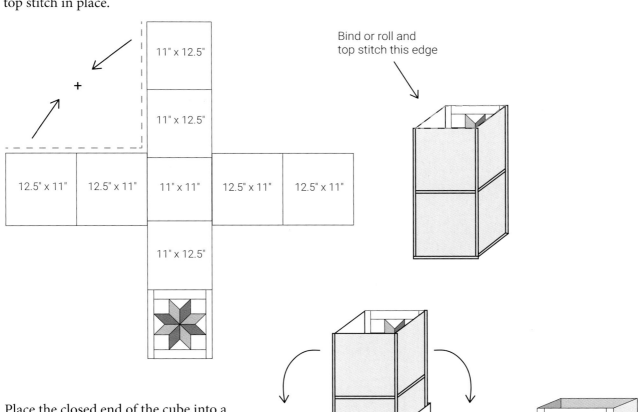

Bind or roll and top stitch this edge

4. Place the closed end of the cube into a bin and pull the edges down over the outside of the bin.

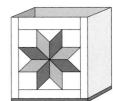

Tumble Quilt

Have you ever admired the look of English Paper Piecing patterns and their shapes, but didn't want to spend the time hand sewing? Y-seams is the answer for you!

  Y-seams enable you to get those fun shapes on a larger scale. The best part of sewing Y-seams is that you don't have to iron or press any seams until you are all done piecing.

Before You Start

Read through all the directions and steps before you start. All seams are sewn with a ¼" seam allowance. **All templates need to be printed at 100%** and *not* "fit to page." You can adjust this in your printer settings. Verify that your template is printed at the correct size by measuring all sides of the 1" reference square.

  For more inspiration, check out the hashtag #tumblequilt and #kileysquiltroom. Be sure to use these when you post pictures of your quilt to share with others!

WOF = Width of Fabric
RST = Right Sides Together

Supplies

Template (page 154)

FABRIC REQUIREMENTS

	Small Throw 45" x 50"	Large Throw 60" x 63"
Colors 1–7	¼ yard each	⅓ yard each
Background	3¼ yards	4¼ yards
Backing	3 yards	3¾ yards
Binding	⅓ yard	½ yard

CUTTING INSTRUCTIONS

	Small Throw 108 Hexagons	Large Throw 195 Hexagons
Colors 1–7	(3) 2¼" x WOF strips of each color	(4) 2¼" x WOF strips of each color
Background	(21) 5¼" x WOF strips	(28) 5¼" x WOF strips

Sew each color fabric strip to a background strip and press toward the background.
See Cutting the Templates (page 108).

Color + Background	Choose 4 fabric colors, cut: (15) *Hexagon Templates* Choose 3 fabric colors, cut: (16) *Hexagon Templates*	Choose 1 fabric color, cut: (27) *Hexagon Templates* Choose 6 fabric colors, cut: (28) *Hexagon Templates*

Line up the seam line with the line on the *Hexagon Template*. Cut around the template. You should be able to get seven hexagons cut out of each strip, as shown.

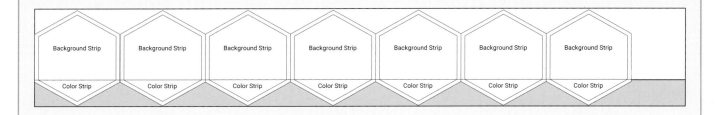

Row Construction

1. Mark a dot on the back of each hexagon that is ¼" from each corner.

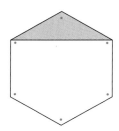

2. Lay out your hexagons. The small throw has 12 rows of 9 hexagons. The large throw has 15 rows of 13 hexagons. See the Quilt Top Reference Chart for which direction each block should face. Space out the colors evenly before you start sewing.

3. Sew your rows together. When joining two hexagons, start and stop on the dots you marked, as shown. Backstitch on both ends for stabilization. Do not press until the end.

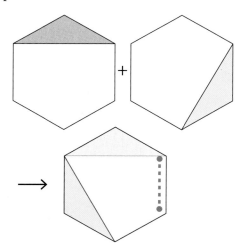

Assembling the Quilt Top

1. Line up the rows so they fit together like a puzzle. You are going to sew one edge at a time. With RST, align the first two edges together and sew. Start and stop ¼" away from the ends. This should meet up with the seams you sewed for the rows.

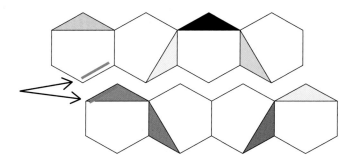

2. Move to the next two edges that line up. With RST, sew them together, starting and stopping ¼" from the ends.

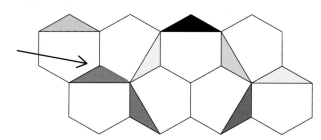

3. Repeat until you have sewn the two rows together. Continue adding rows until your quilt top is complete.

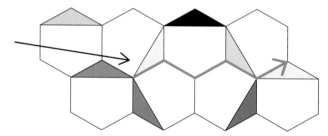

4. It's time to press. Your intersecting seams need to look like a pinwheel. To do this, all seams that intersect should follow in the same direction as the last seam you pressed, kind of like following a circular path. Each intersection will do this, so make sure that, from one intersection to the next, the seams are still following this pattern.

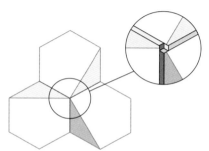

Back of Quilt

Quilt Top Reference Chart

Use this layout as a reference for arranging your hexagons to get the desired pattern for this Tumble Quilt design.

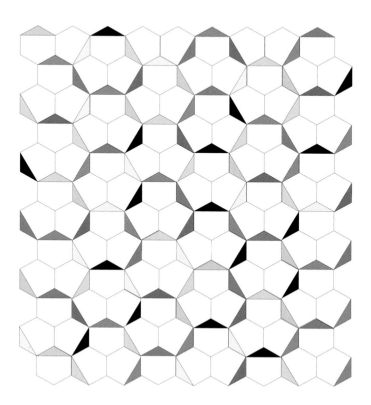

Take your time pressing the pinwheel seams. It will make a big difference in keeping the blocks flat.

Templates

Countdown Chain Template

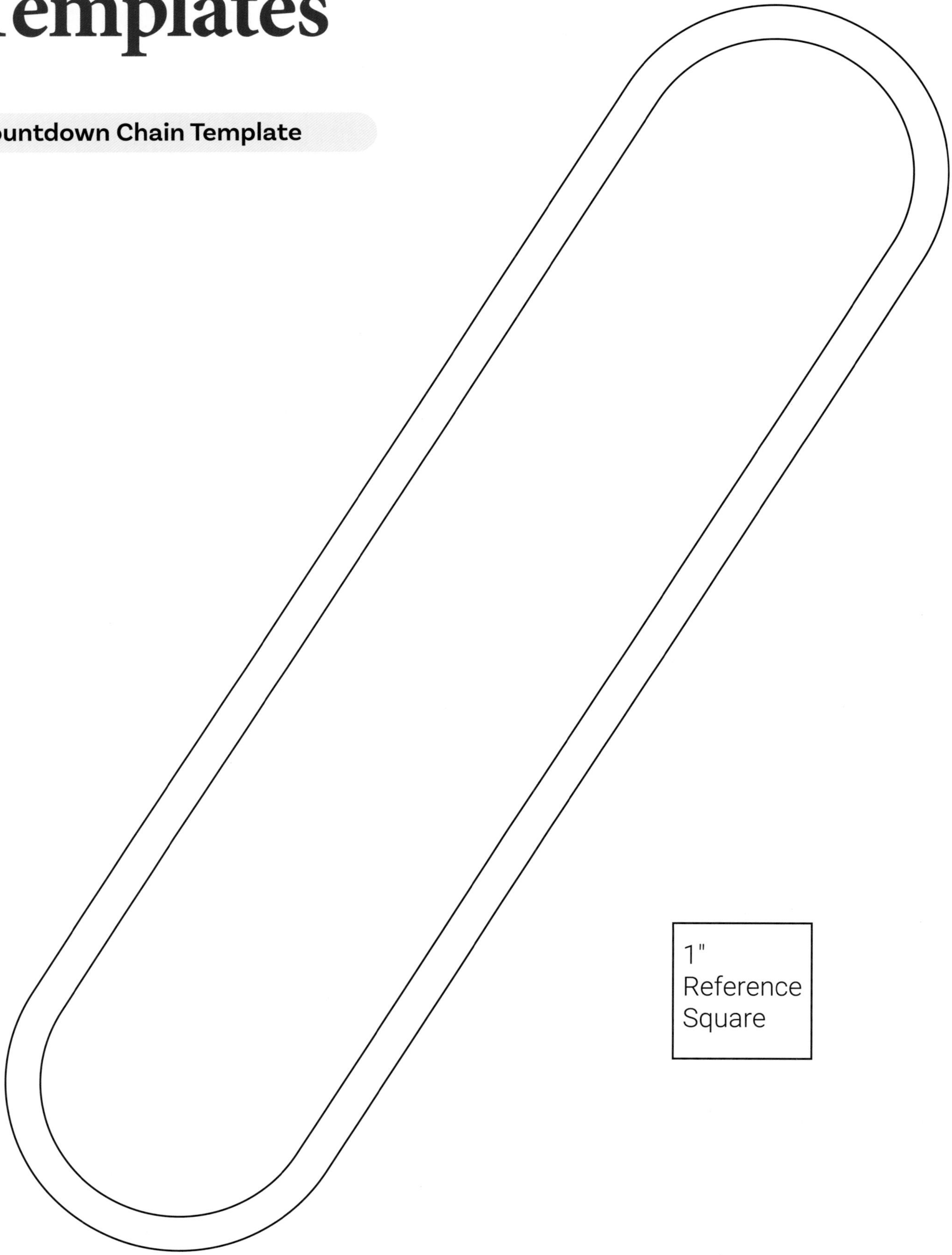

1"
Reference
Square

Rope Swing Templates

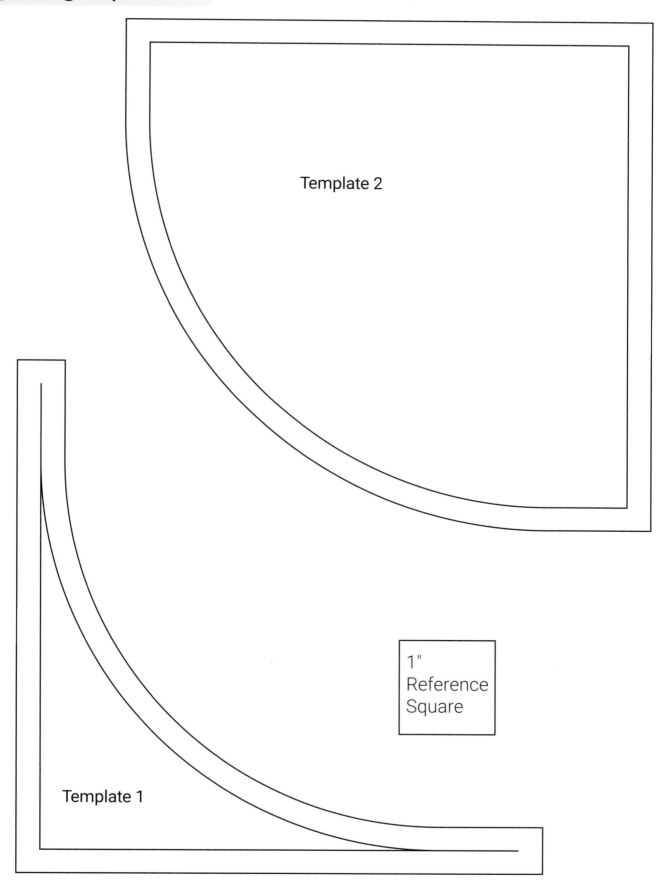

Template 2

1"
Reference
Square

Template 1

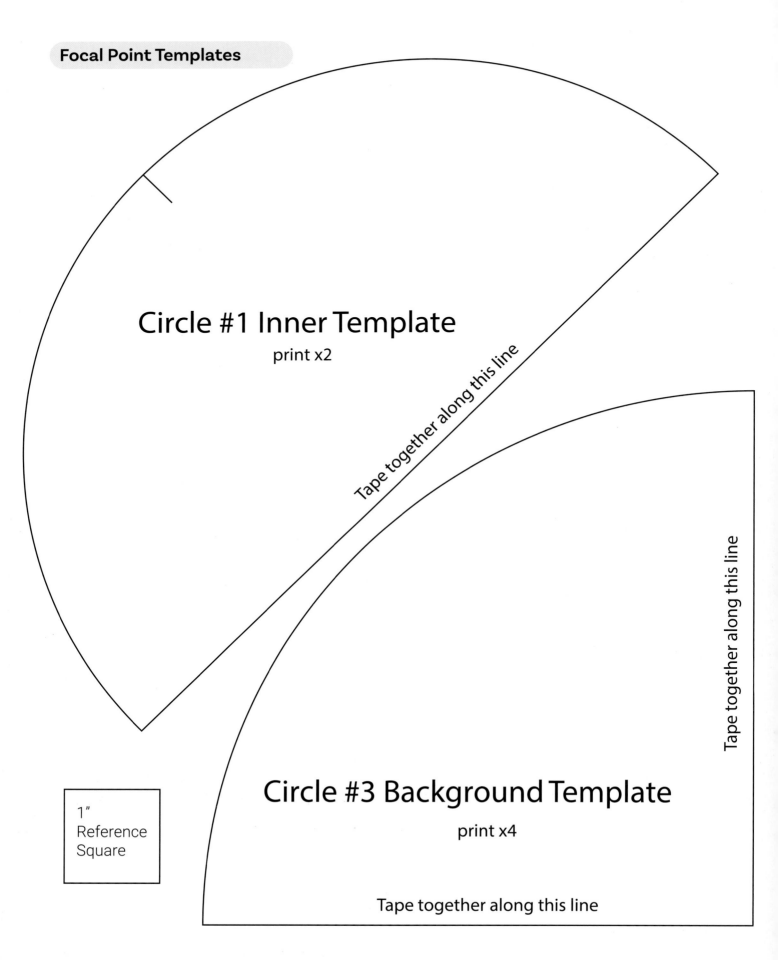

Circle #1 Inner Template

print x2

Tape together along this line

Circle #3 Background Template

print x4

Tape together along this line

Tape together along this line

1"
Reference
Square

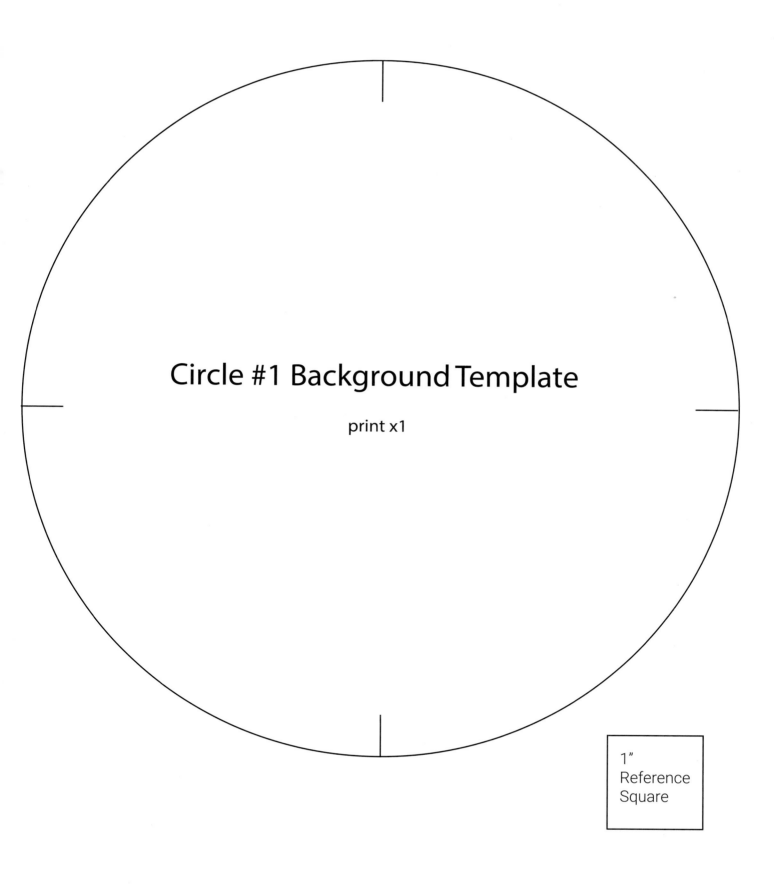

Circle #1 Background Template

print x1

1"
Reference
Square

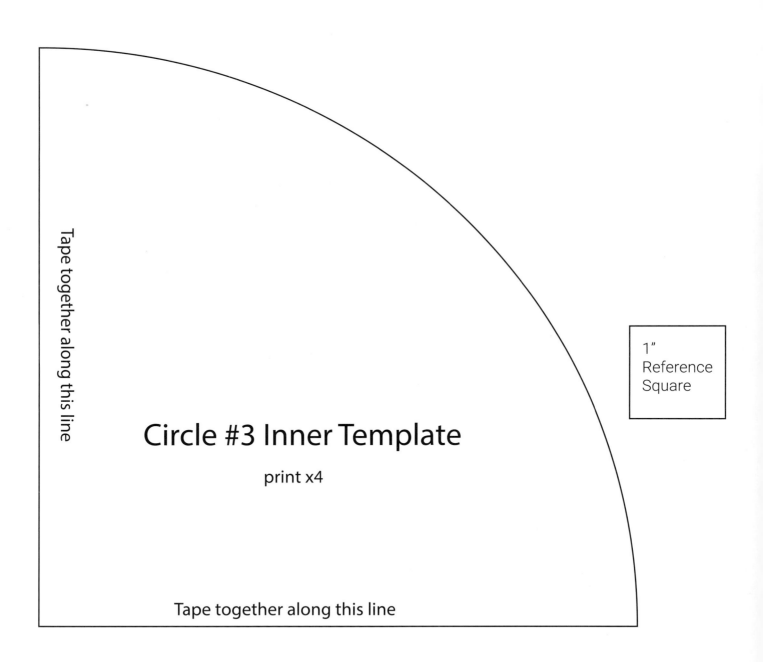

Tape together along this line

Circle #3 Inner Template

print x4

Tape together along this line

1"
Reference
Square

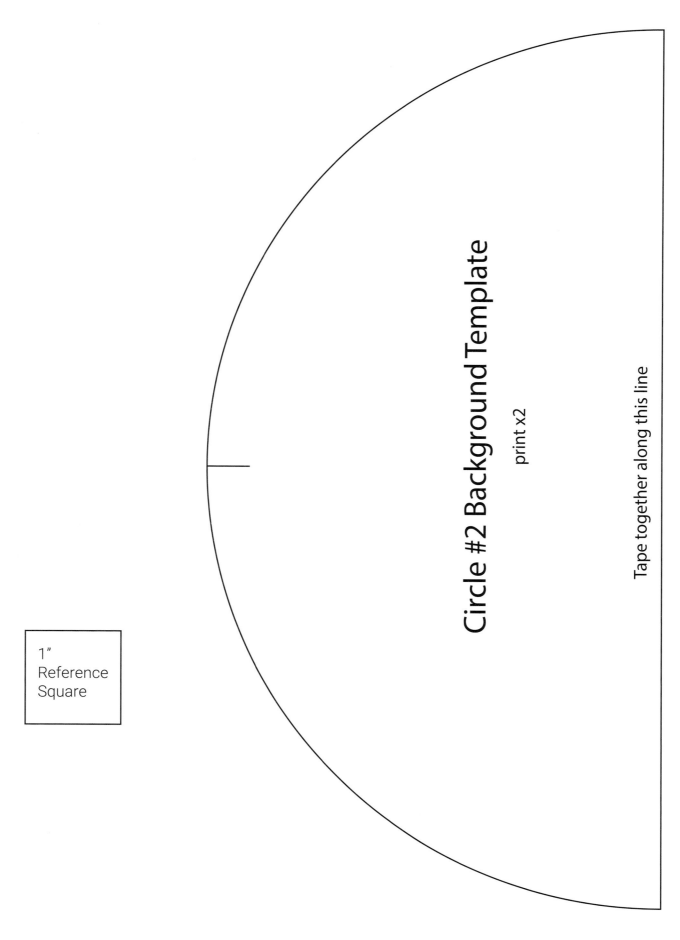

Circle #2 Background Template

print x2

Tape together along this line

1"
Reference
Square

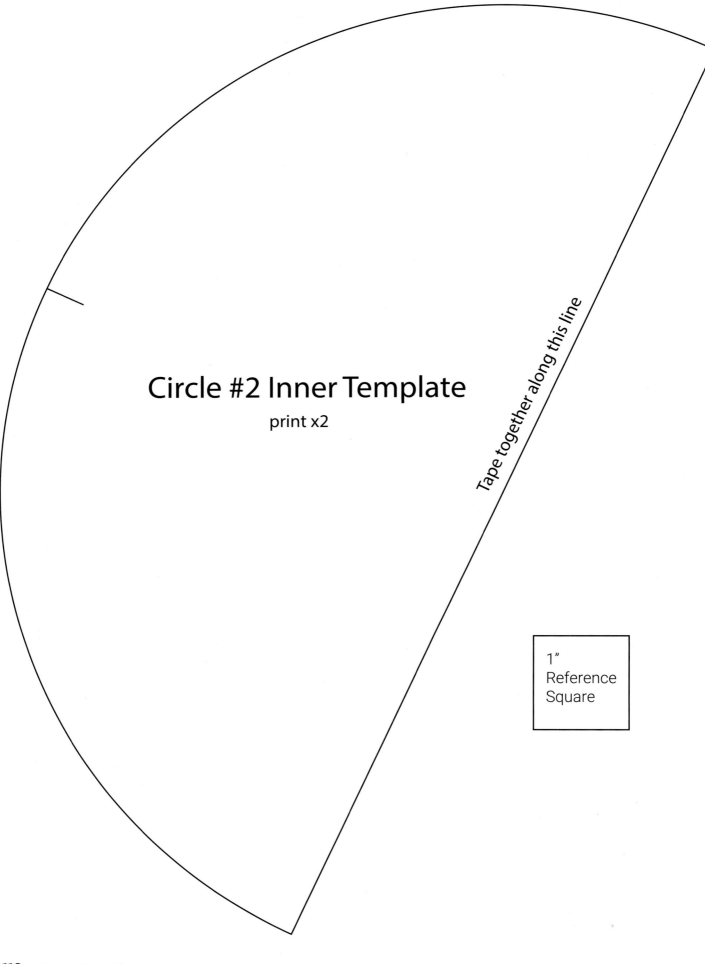

Circle #2 Inner Template

print x2

Tape together along this line

1"
Reference
Square

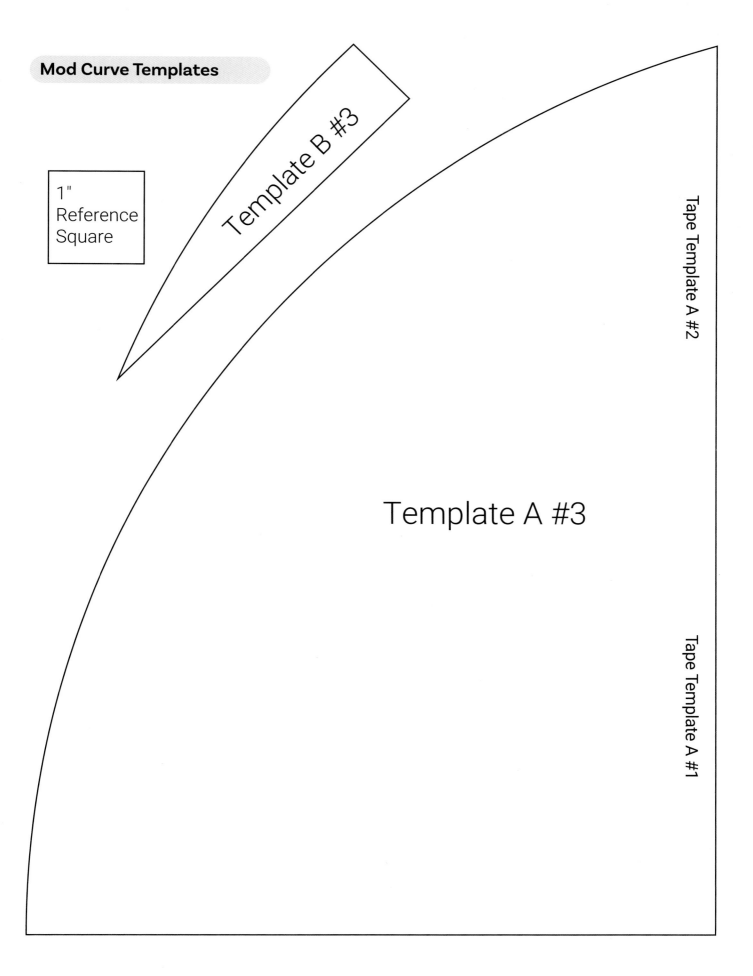

Mod Curve Templates

1"
Reference
Square

Template B #3

Template A #3

Tape Template A #2

Tape Template A #1

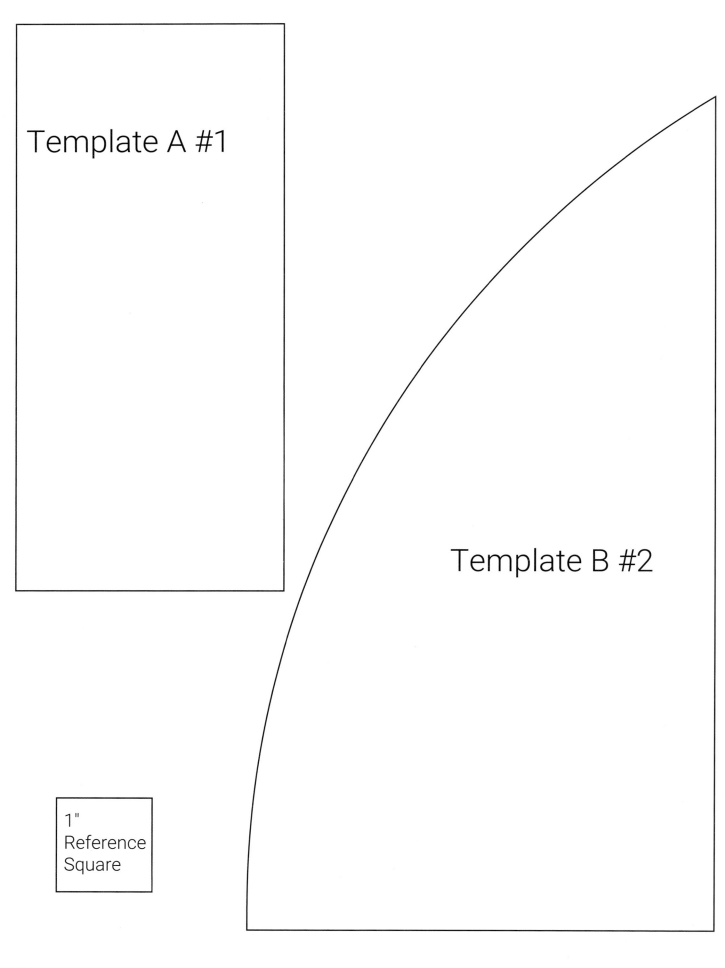

Template A #1

Template B #2

1"
Reference
Square

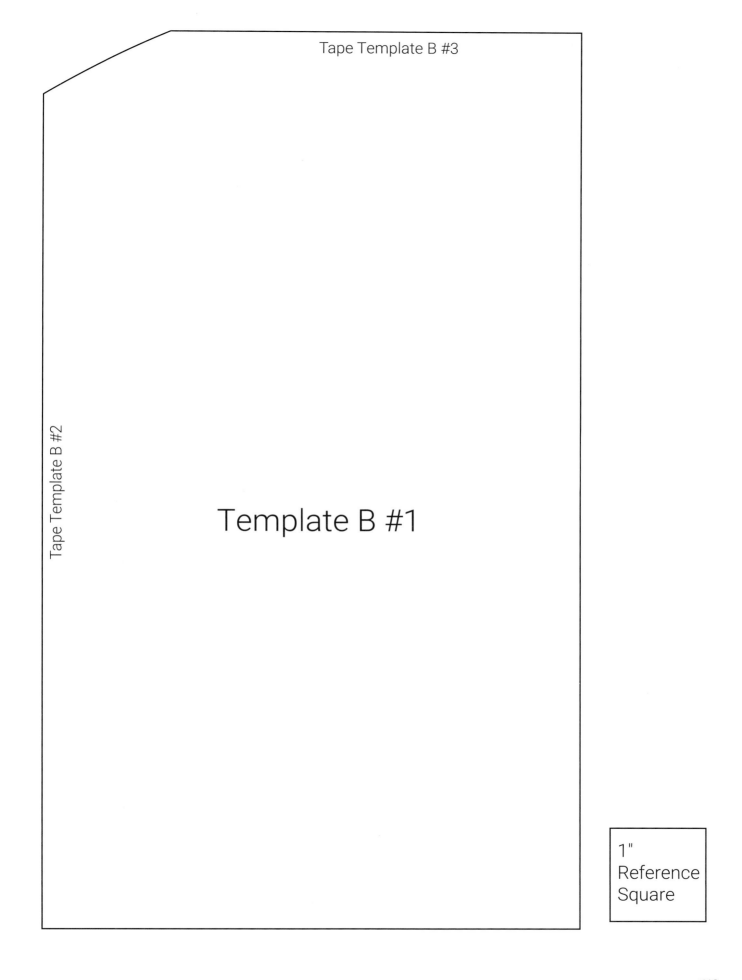

Tape Template B #3

Tape Template B #2

Template B #1

1"
Reference
Square

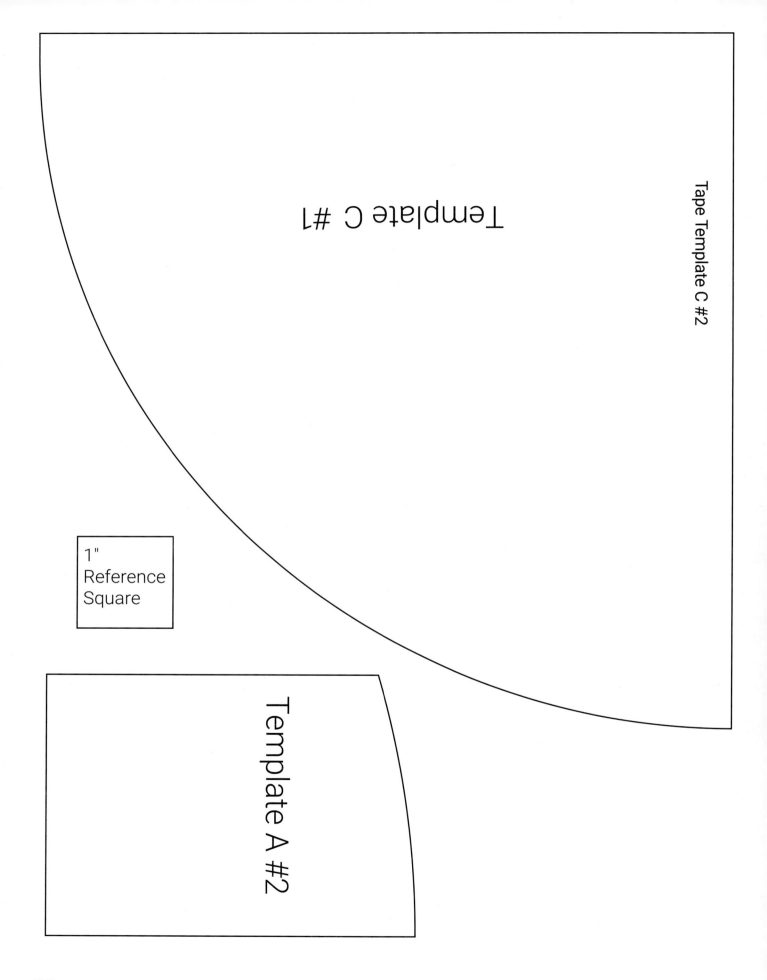

Tape Template C #2

Template C #1

1"
Reference
Square

Template A #2

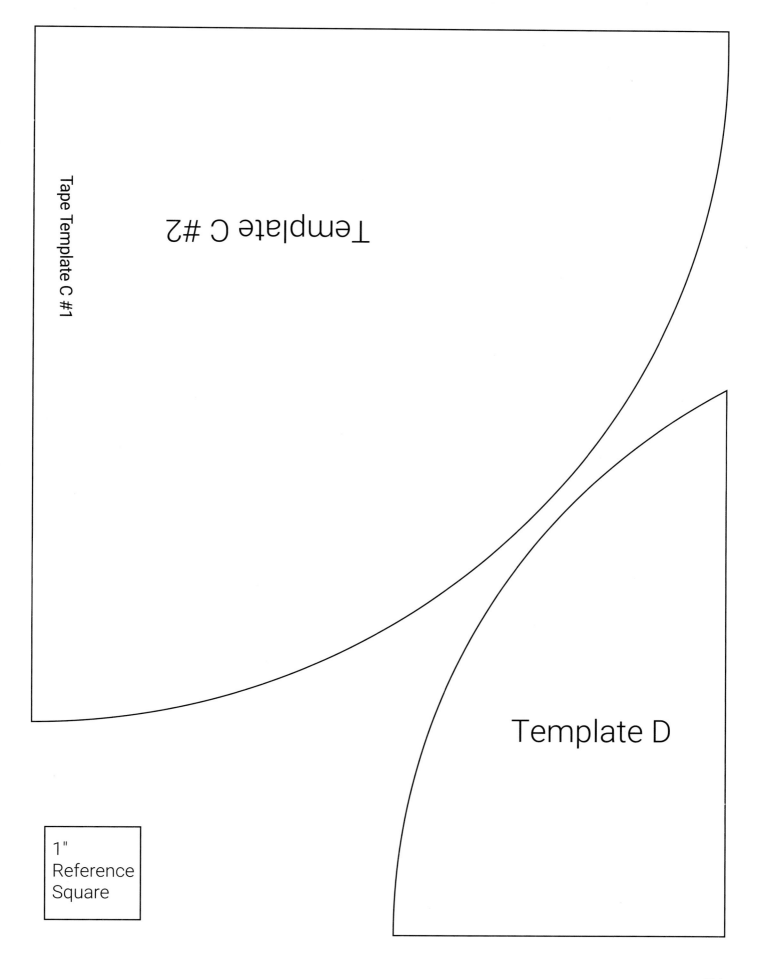

Tape Template C #1

Template C #2

Template D

1"
Reference
Square

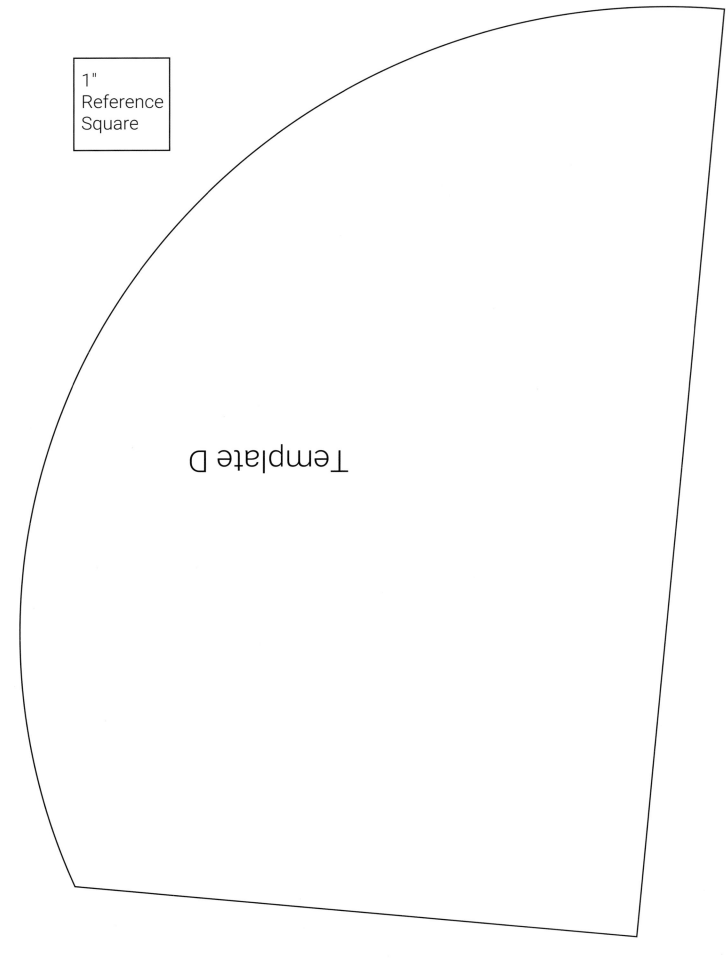

1"
Reference
Square

Template D

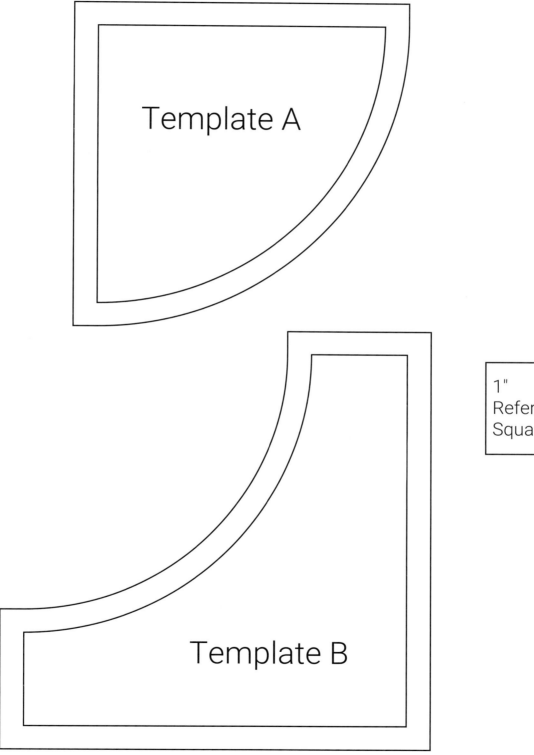

Template A

Template B

1"
Reference
Square

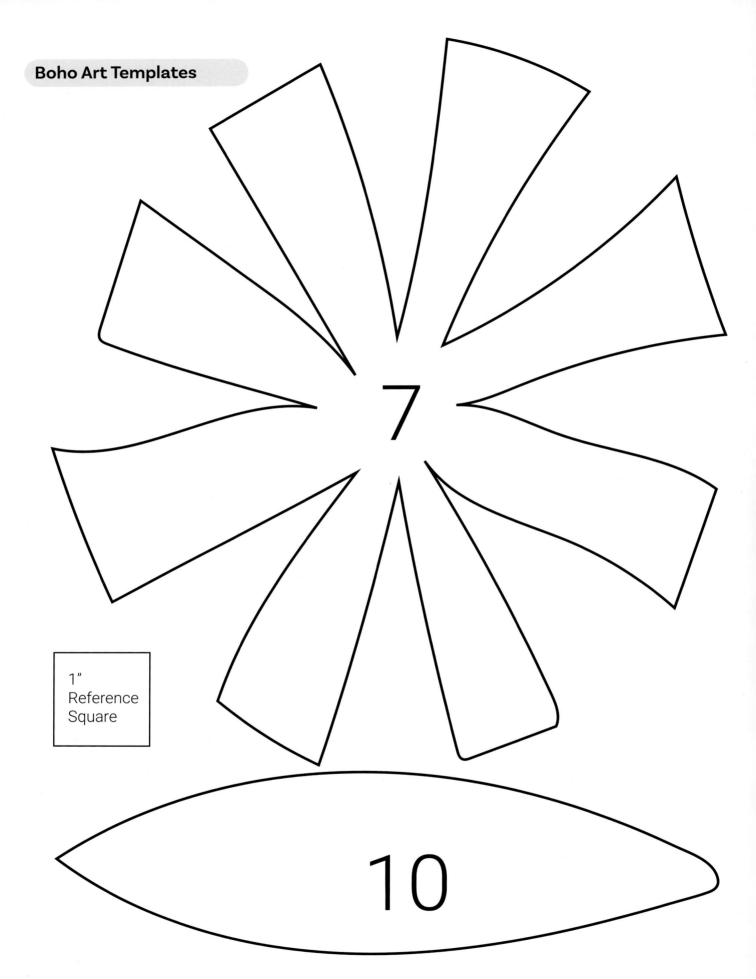

1"
Reference
Square

7

10

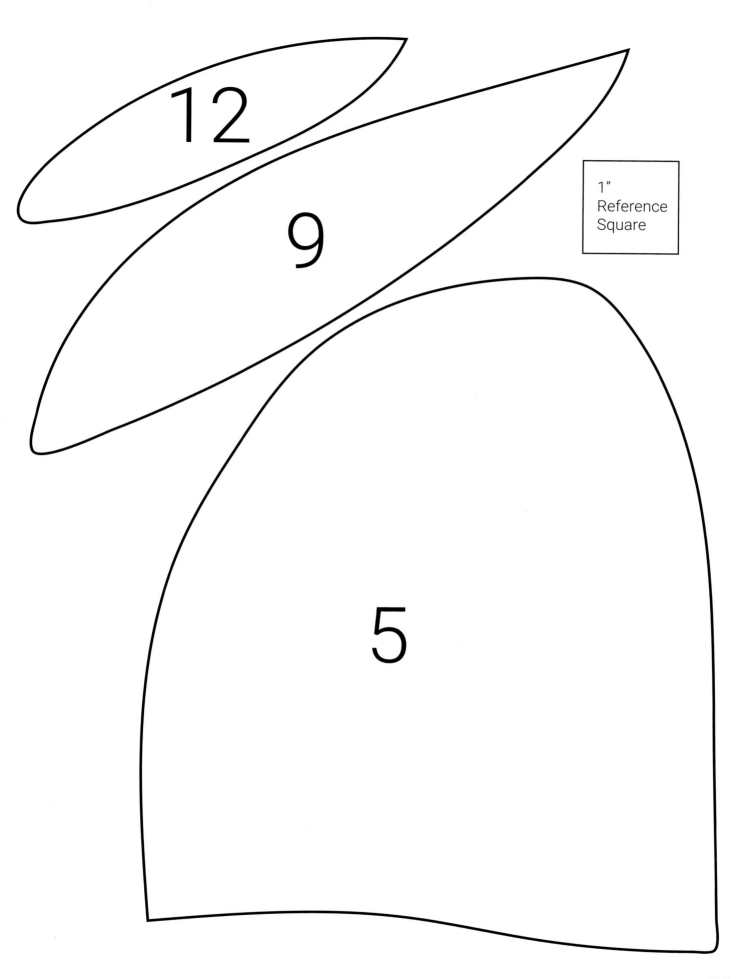

12

9

1"
Reference
Square

5

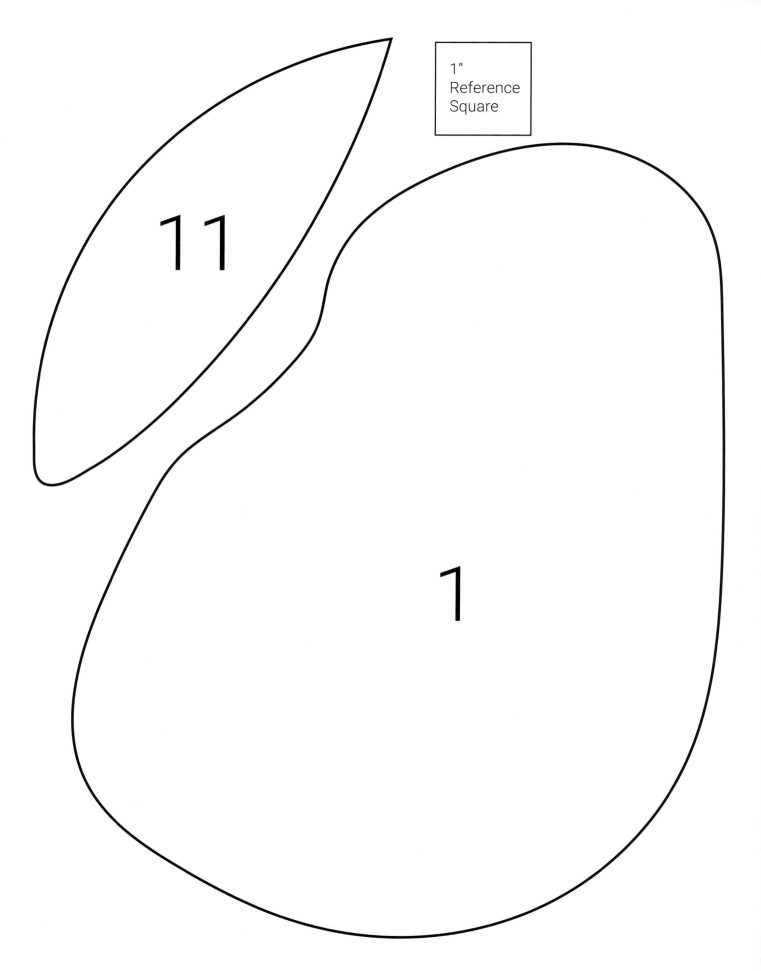

1"
Reference
Square

11

1

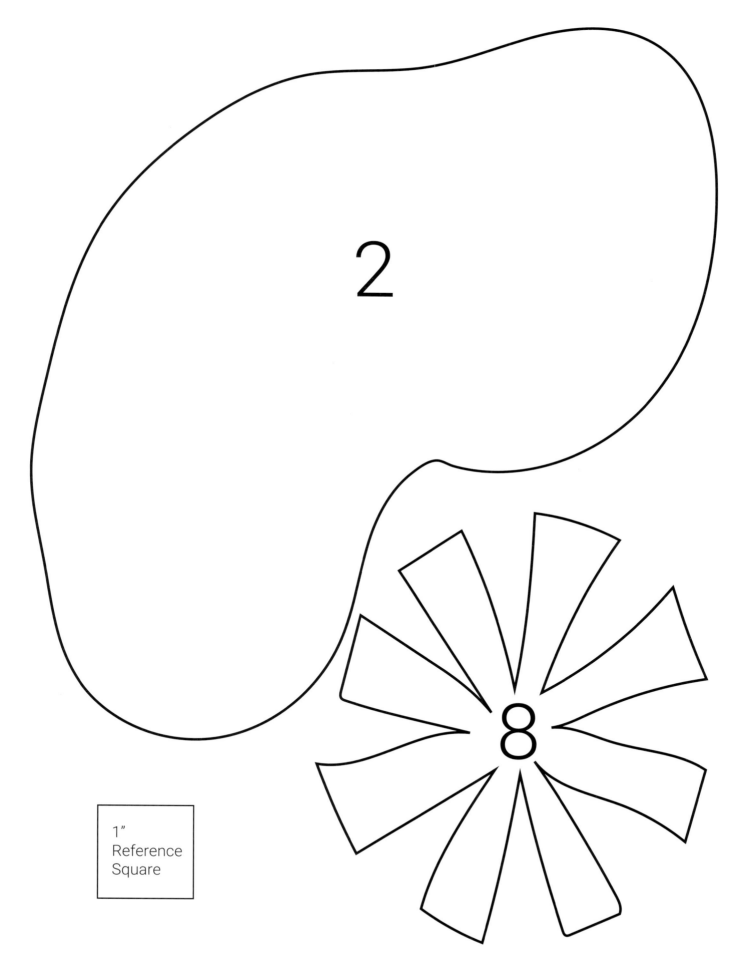

2

8

1"
Reference
Square

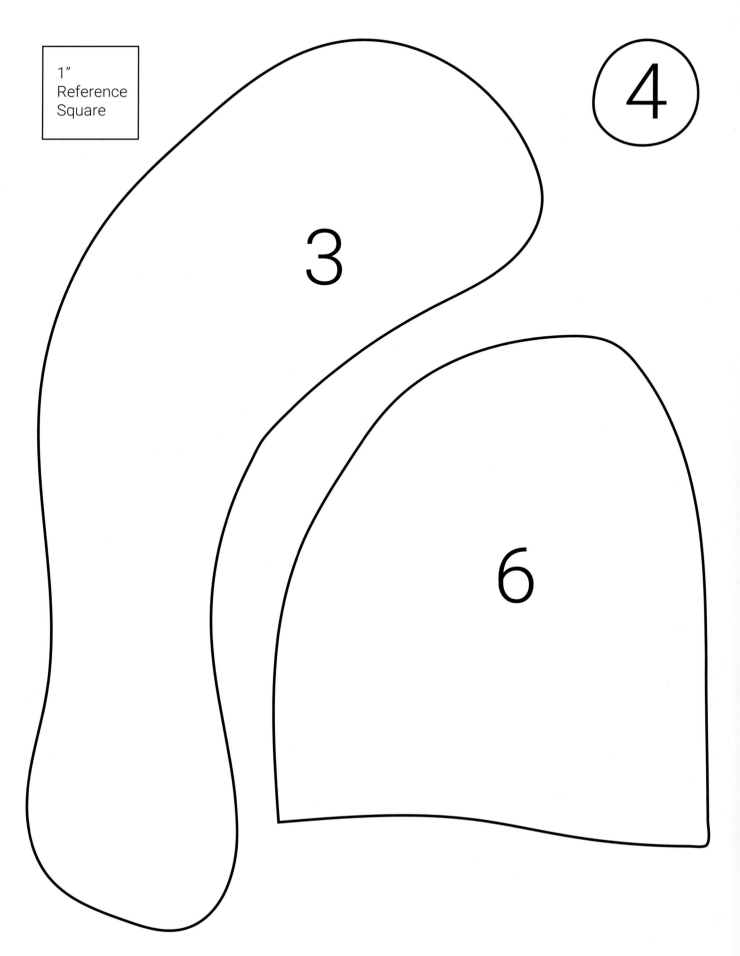

1"
Reference
Square

4

3

6

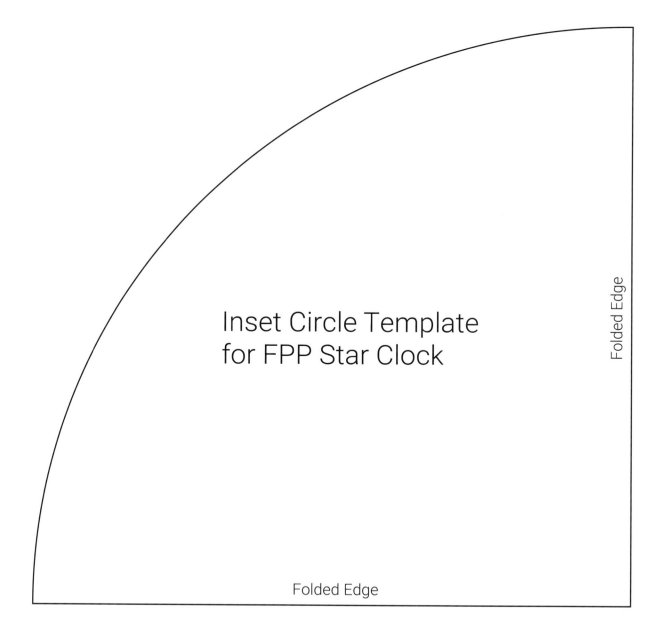

1"
Reference
Square

Inset Circle Template
for FPP Star Clock

Folded Edge

Folded Edge

Print this page 4 times to get 12 sections of the clock circle.

1"
Reference
Square

Jack-O-Quilt Templates

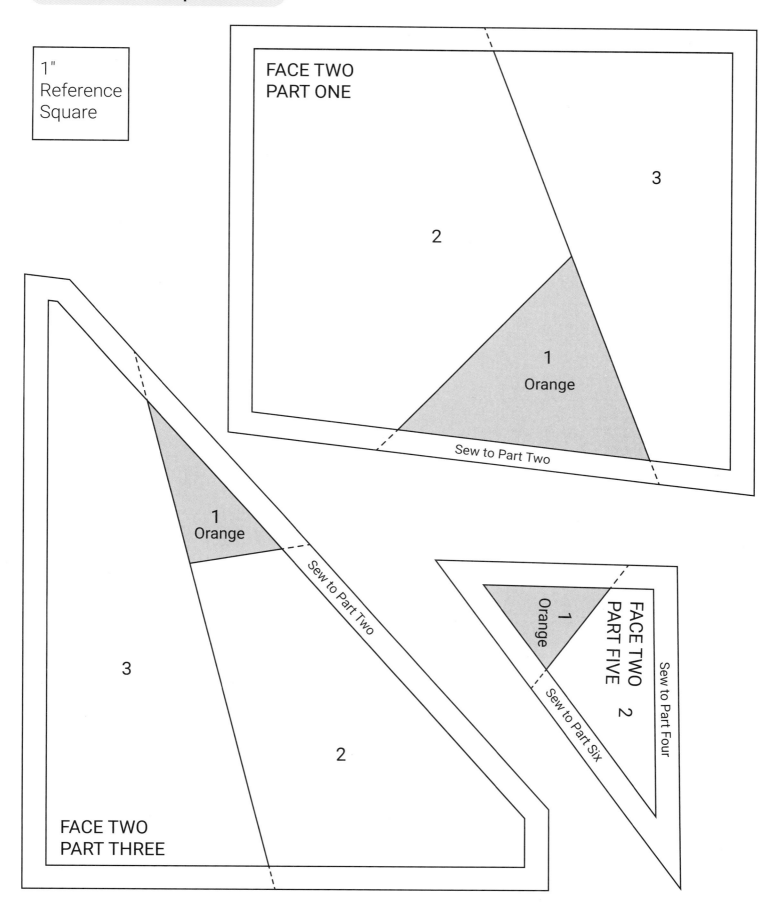

1"
Reference
Square

FACE TWO
PART ONE

3

2

1
Orange

Sew to Part Two

1
Orange

Sew to Part Two

3

2

FACE TWO
PART THREE

1
Orange

FACE TWO
PART FIVE

2

Sew to Part Six

Sew to Part Four

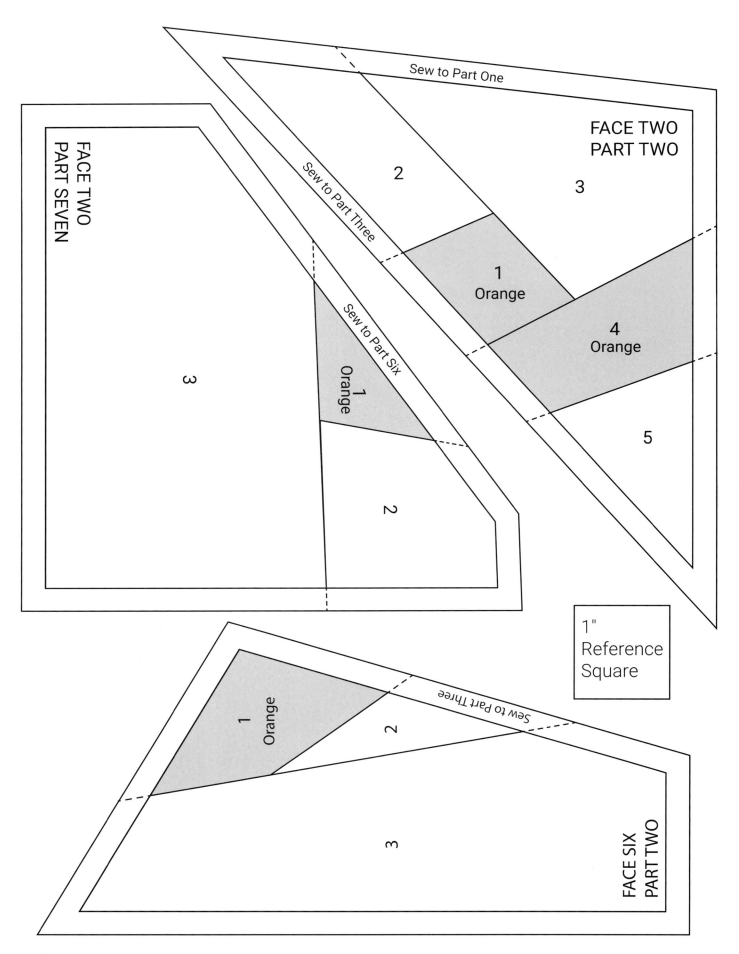

FACE TWO
PART TWO

Sew to Part One

2

3

Sew to Part Three

1
Orange

4
Orange

5

FACE TWO
PART SEVEN

3

Sew to Part Six

1
Orange

2

1"
Reference
Square

Sew to Part Three

1
Orange

2

3

FACE SIX
PART TWO

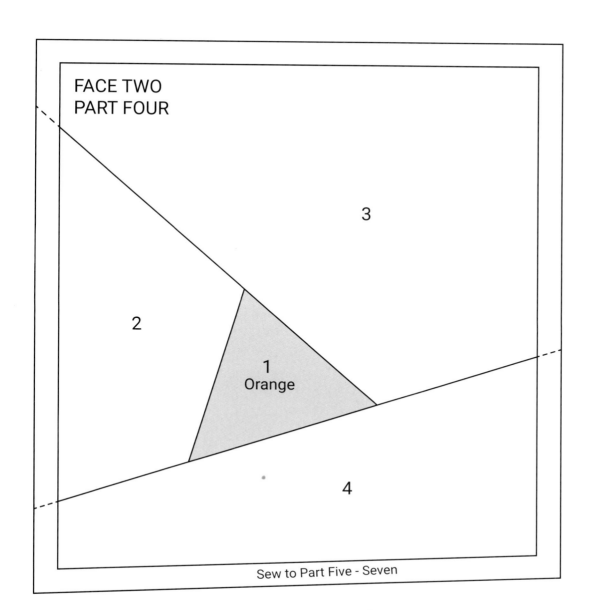

FACE TWO
PART FOUR

3

2

1
Orange

4

Sew to Part Five - Seven

1"
Reference
Square

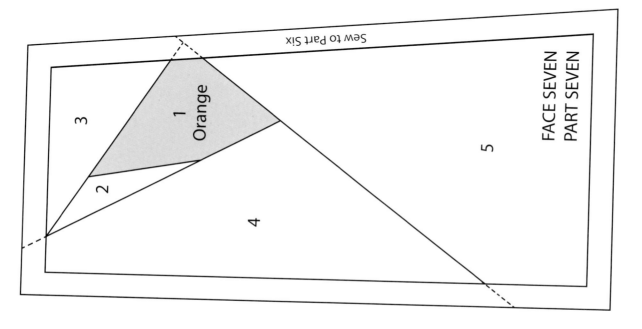

Sew to Part Six

3

1
Orange

2

4

5

FACE SEVEN
PART SEVEN

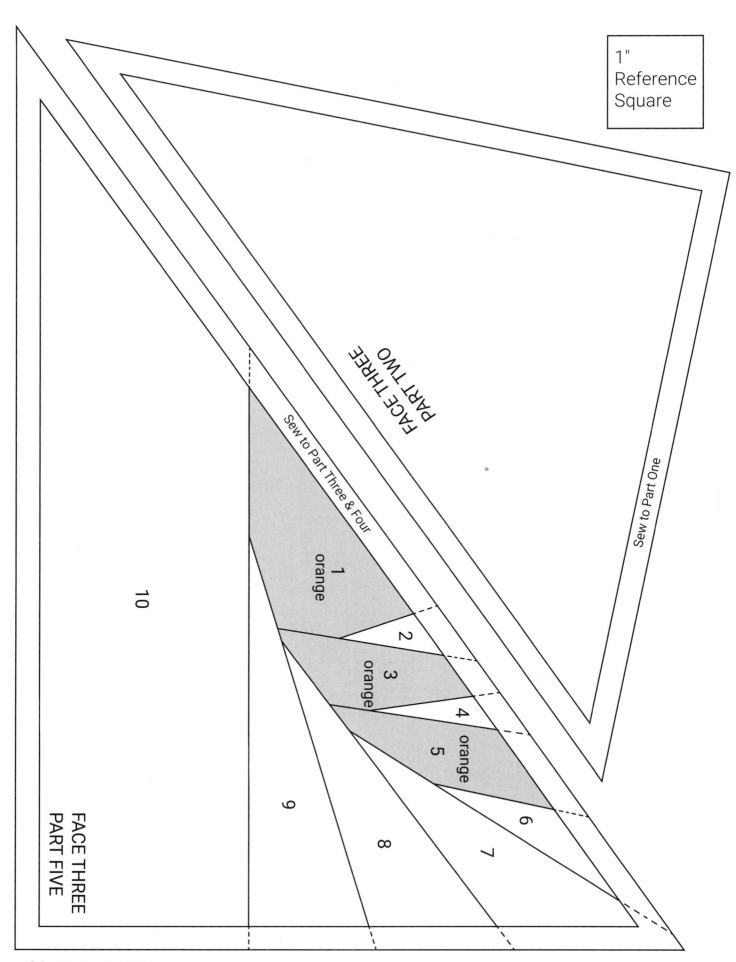

1"
Reference
Square

FACE THREE
PART TWO

Sew to Part One

Sew to Part Three & Four

1
orange

2

3
orange

4

orange

5

6

7

8

9

10

FACE THREE
PART FIVE

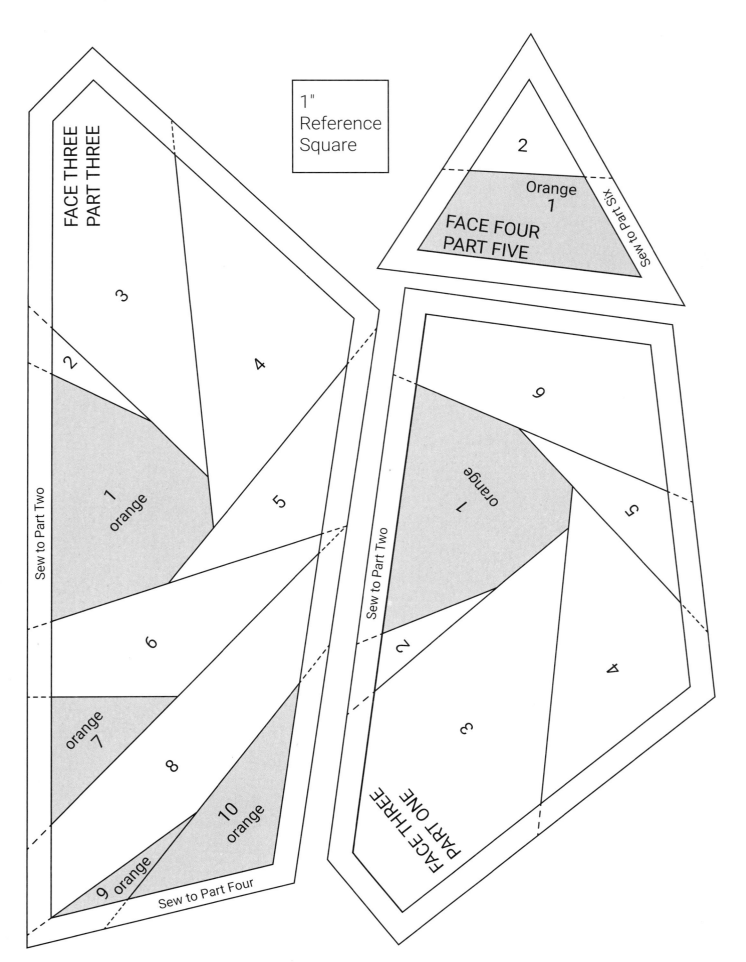

1"
Reference
Square

FACE THREE
PART THREE

FACE FOUR
PART FIVE

Orange
1

2

Sew to Part Six

3

2

4

1
orange

5

Sew to Part Two

6

orange
7

8

10
orange

9 orange

Sew to Part Four

9

orange
1

5

2

4

3

Sew to Part Two

FACE THREE
PART ONE

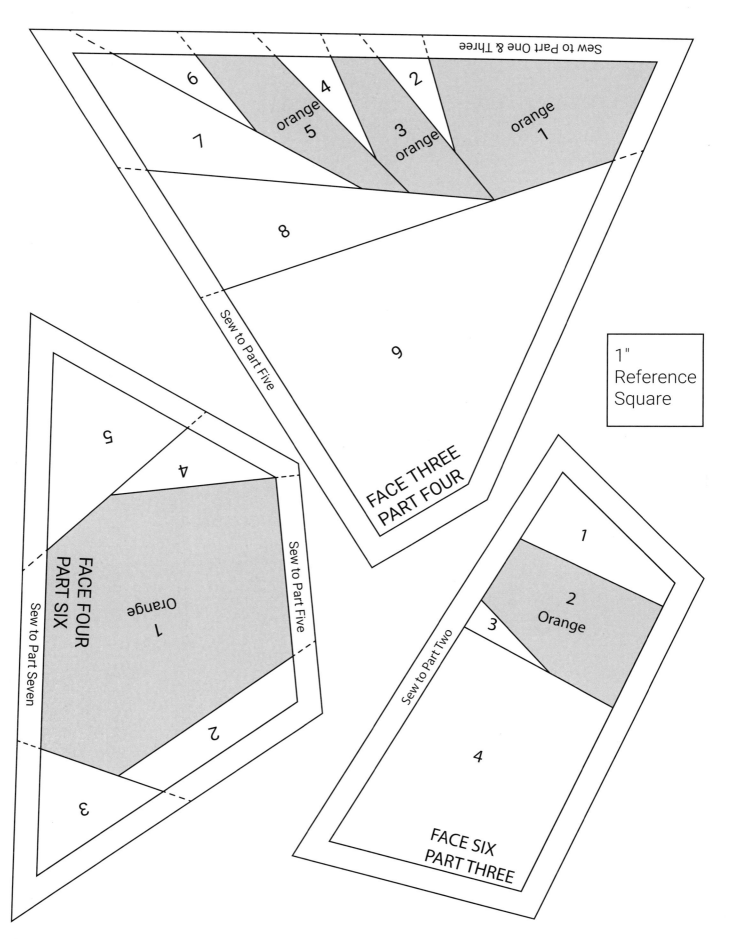

1"
Reference
Square

Sew to Part One & Three

orange 1

2

orange 3

4

orange 5

6

7

8

9

FACE THREE
PART FOUR

Sew to Part Five

5

4

Sew to Part Five

Orange 1

FACE FOUR
PART SIX

2

3

Sew to Part Seven

1

2
Orange

3

Sew to Part Two

4

FACE SIX
PART THREE

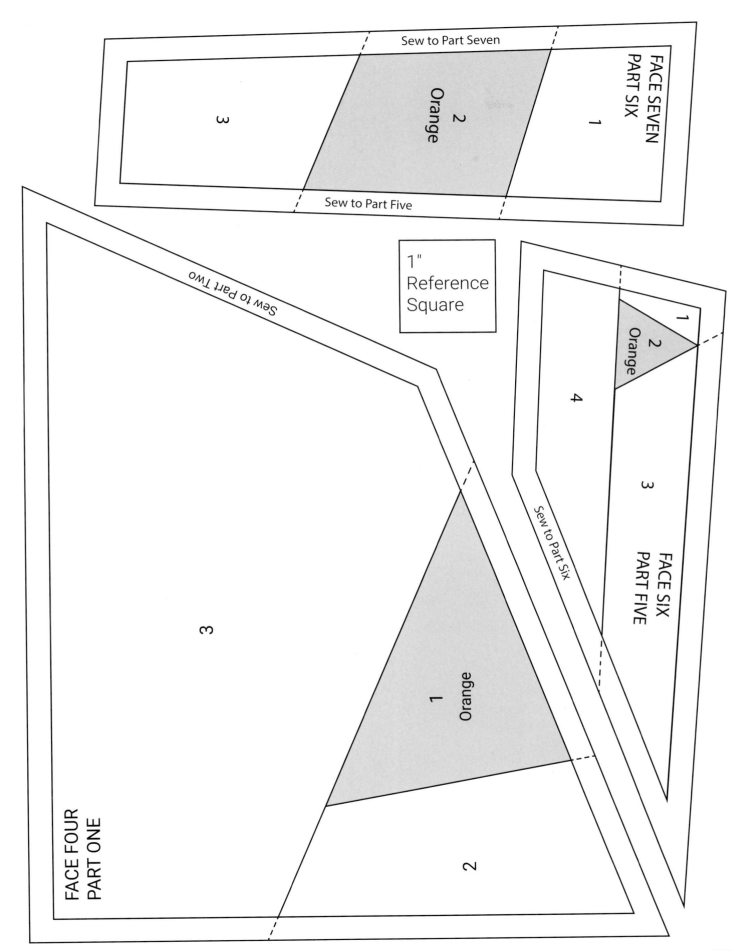

FACE SEVEN
PART SIX

3

2
Orange

1

Sew to Part Seven

Sew to Part Five

1"
Reference
Square

FACE SIX
PART FIVE

1

2
Orange

4

3

2

FACE FOUR
PART ONE

Sew to Part Two

Sew to Part Six

3

Orange
1

2

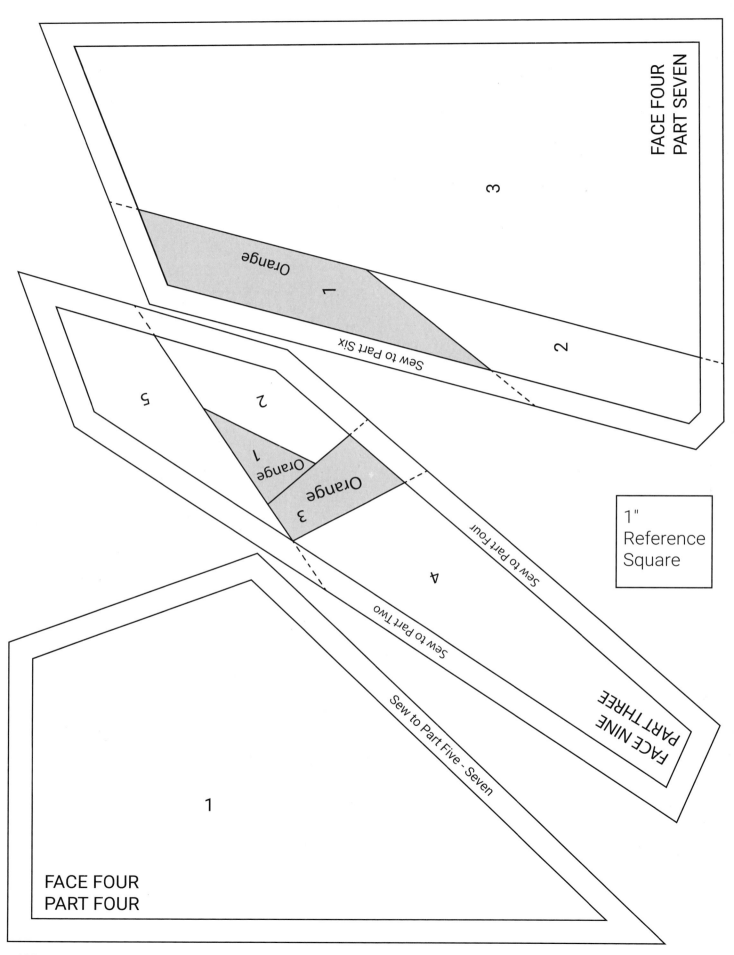

FACE FOUR
PART SEVEN

3

Orange

1

2

Sew to Part Six

5

2

Orange

1

Orange

3

Sew to Part Four

4

Sew to Part Two

1"
Reference
Square

FACE NINE
PART THREE

Sew to Part Five - Seven

FACE FOUR
PART FOUR

1

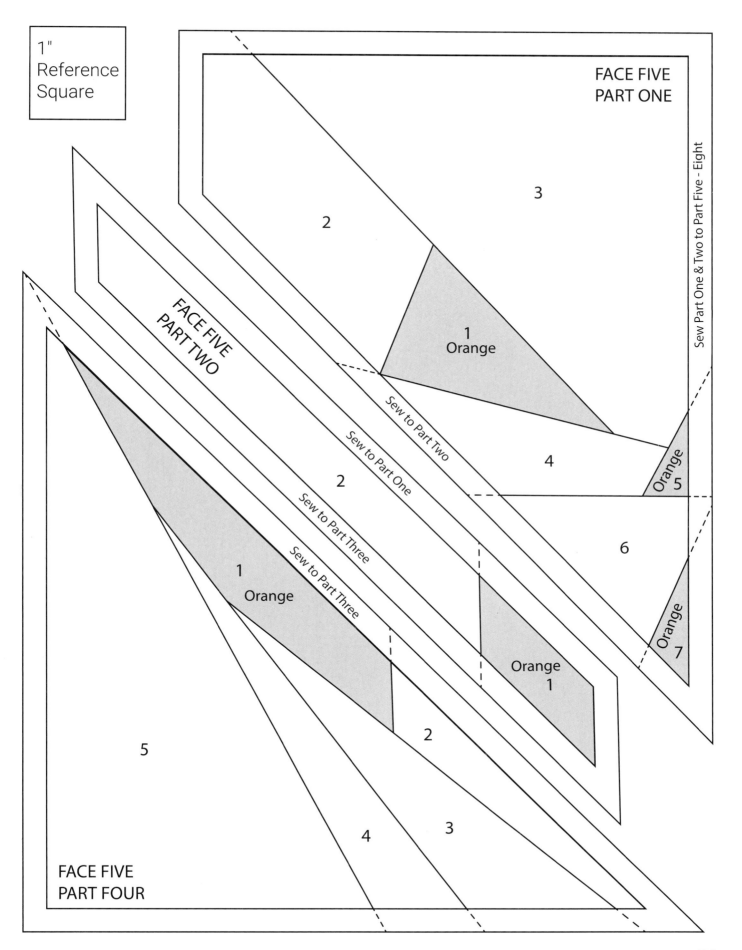

1"
Reference
Square

FACE FIVE
PART ONE

Sew Part One & Two to Part Five - Eight

3

2

1
Orange

Sew to Part Two

Sew to Part One

FACE FIVE
PART TWO

4

Orange
5

2

6

Sew to Part Three

Sew to Part Three

1
Orange

Orange
7

Orange
1

2

5

3

4

FACE FIVE
PART FOUR

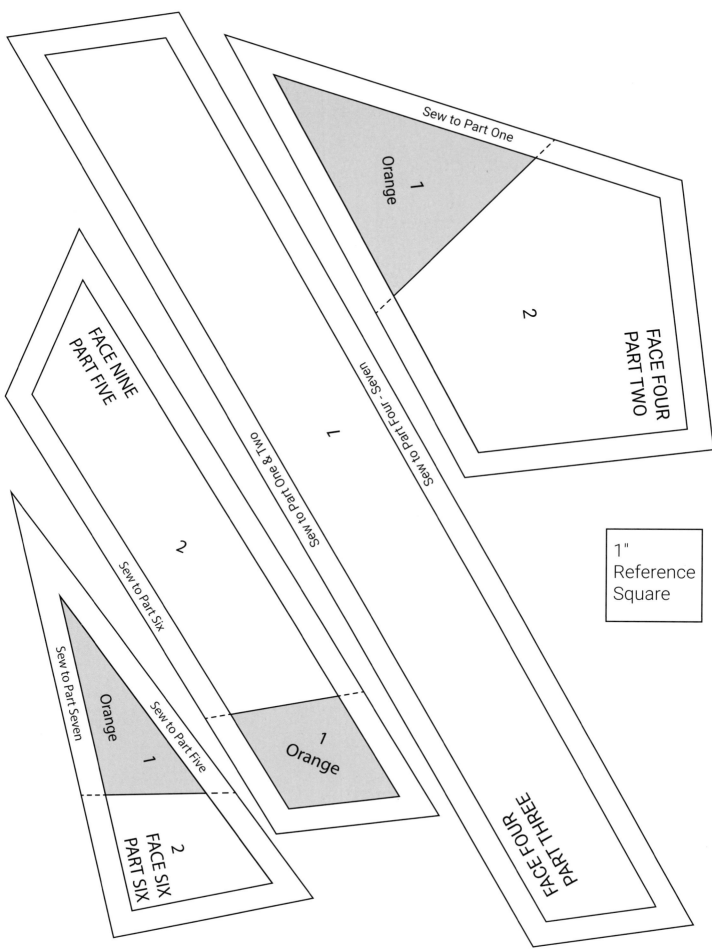

FACE FOUR
PART TWO

Sew to Part One

1
Orange

2

Sew to Part Four - Seven

FACE NINE
PART FIVE

Sew to Part One & Two

1

2

Sew to Part Six

1"
Reference
Square

FACE FOUR
PART THREE

Sew to Part Five

Sew to Part Seven

Orange
1

1
Orange

2
FACE SIX
PART SIX

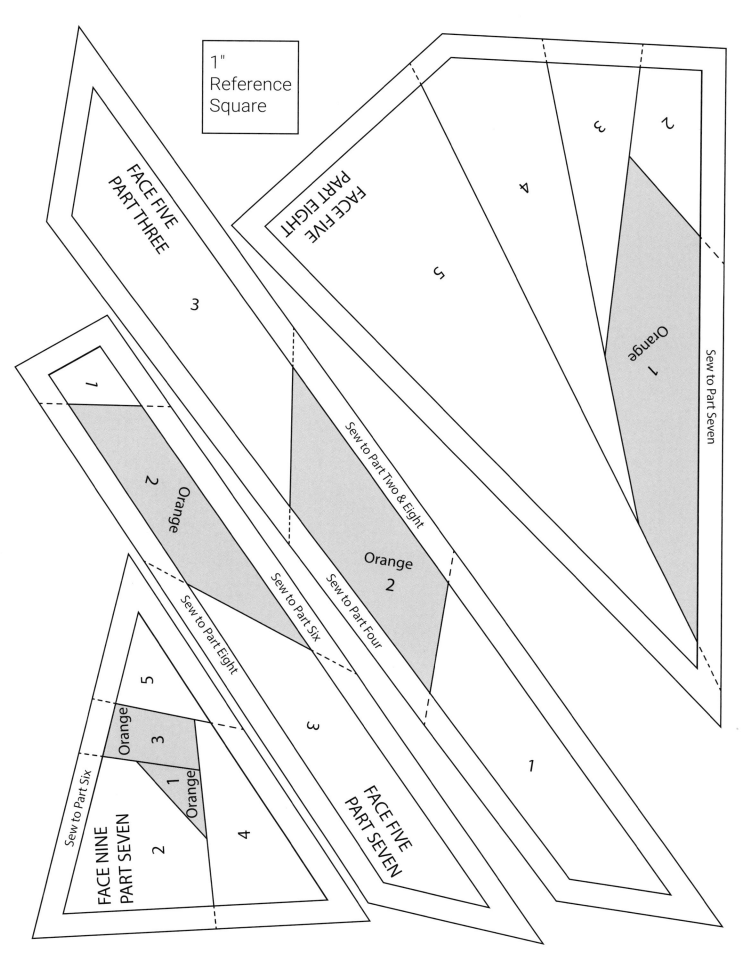

1"
Reference
Square

FACE FIVE
PART THREE

3

1

Orange
2

Orange

FACE FIVE
PART EIGHT

3

2

4

5

1
Orange

Sew to Part Seven

Sew to Part Two & Eight

Sew to Part Four

Orange
2

Sew to Part Six

Sew to Part Eight

3

1

FACE FIVE
PART SEVEN

5

Orange
3

Orange
1

Sew to Part Six

2

4

FACE NINE
PART SEVEN

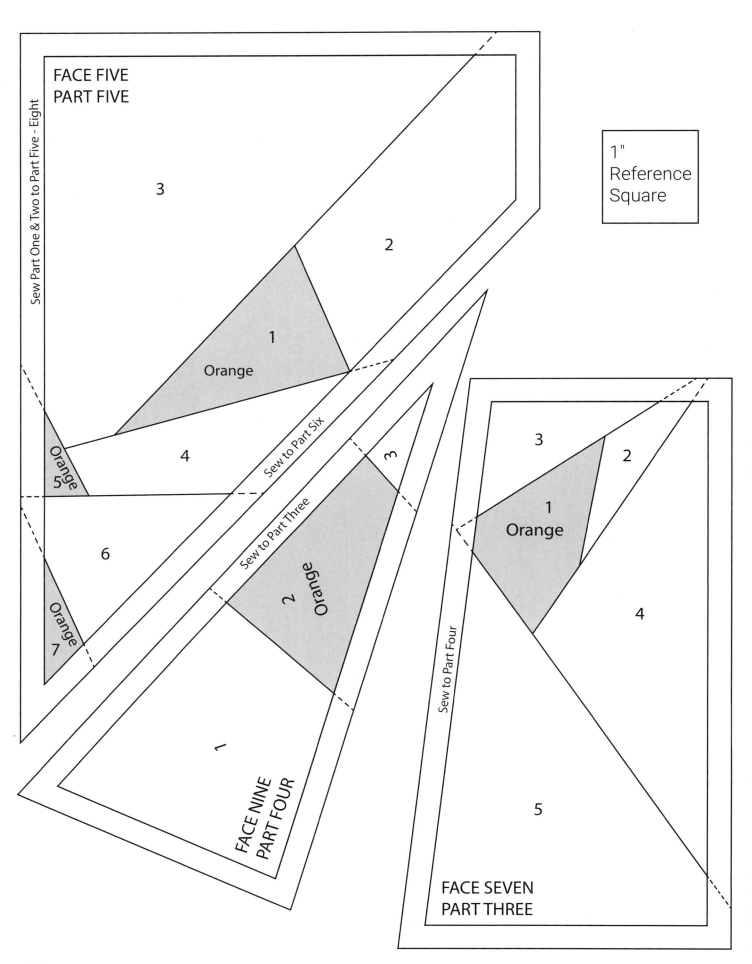

FACE FIVE
PART FIVE

Sew Part One & Two to Part Five - Eight

3

2

1
Orange

Sew to Part Six

Sew to Part Three

Orange
5

4

3

6

2
Orange

Orange
7

Sew to Part Four

1

FACE NINE
PART FOUR

1" Reference Square

3

2

1
Orange

4

5

FACE SEVEN
PART THREE

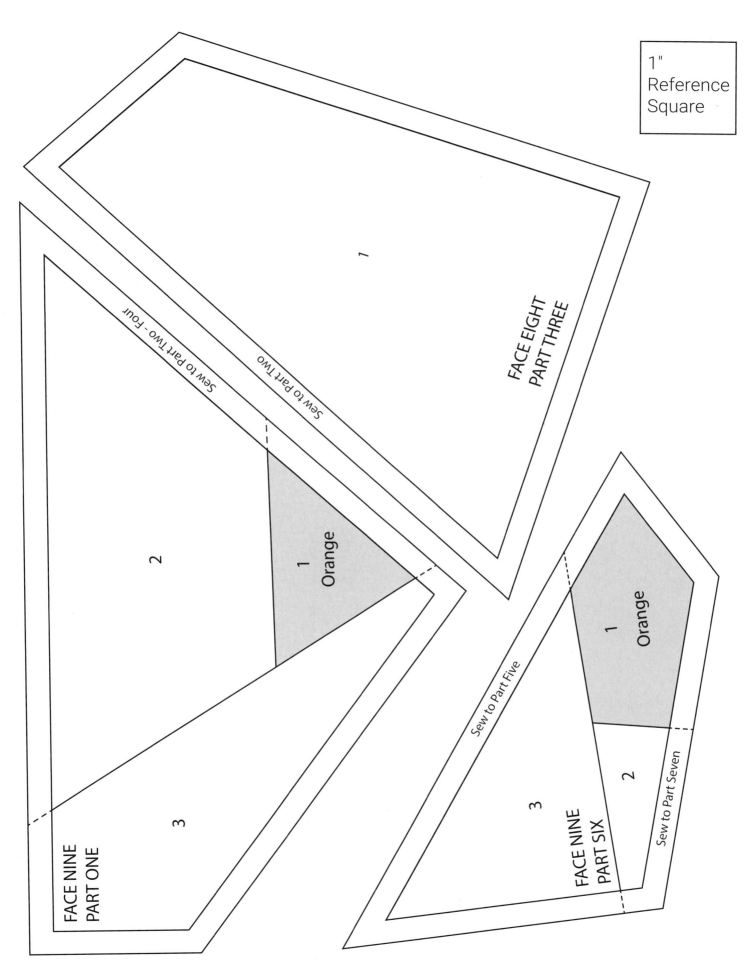

1" Reference Square

FACE EIGHT
PART THREE

1

Sew to Part Two - Four

Sew to Part Two

2

1
Orange

FACE NINE
PART ONE

3

Sew to Part Five

1
Orange

2

Sew to Part Seven

3

FACE NINE
PART SIX

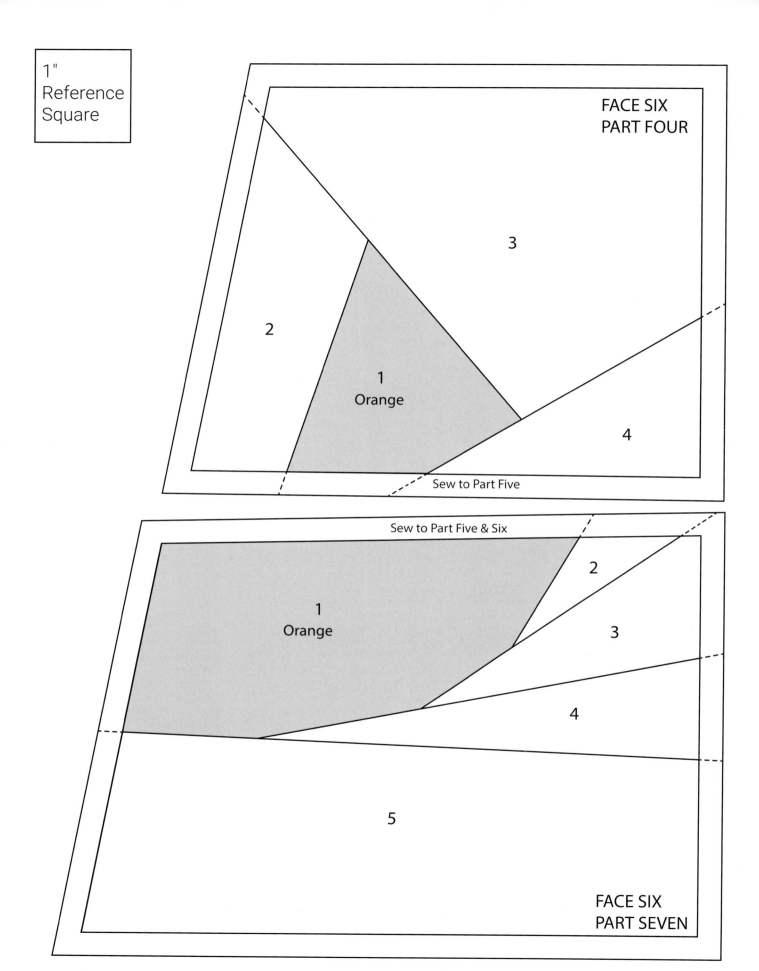

1" Reference Square

FACE SIX
PART FOUR

3

2

1
Orange

4

Sew to Part Five

Sew to Part Five & Six

1
Orange

2

3

4

5

FACE SIX
PART SEVEN

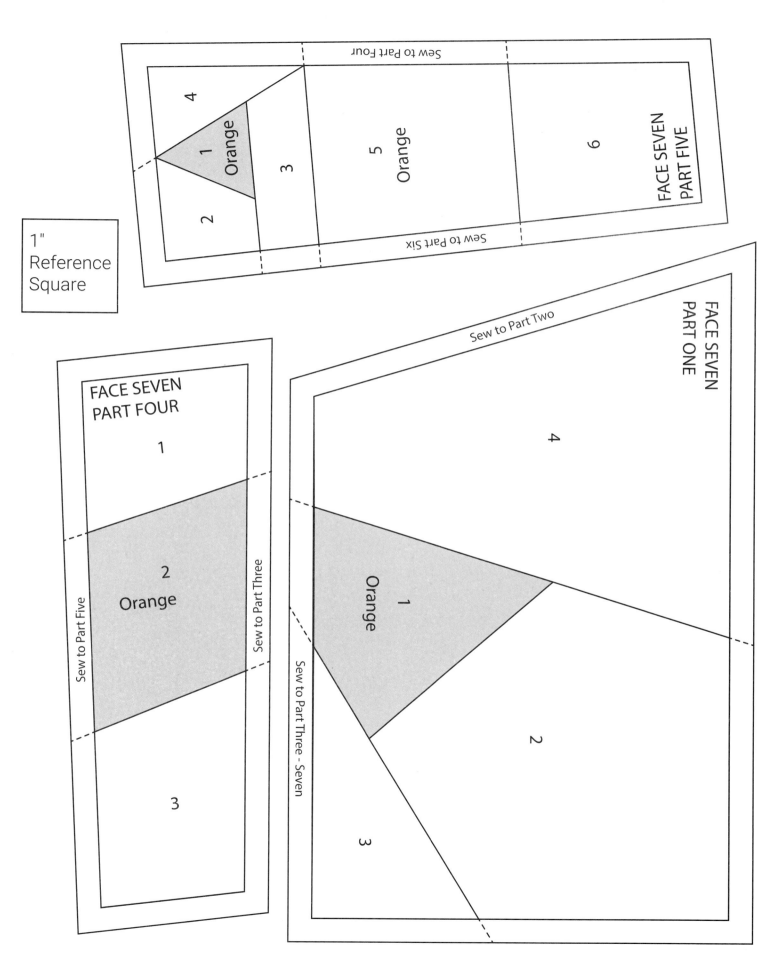

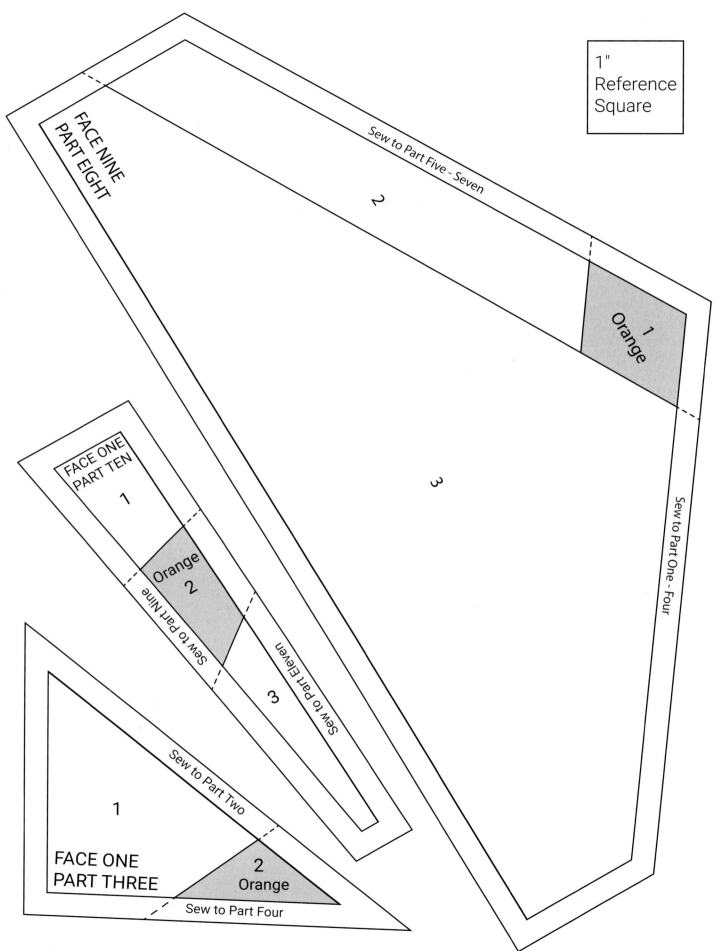

1"
Reference
Square

FACE NINE
PART EIGHT

Sew to Part Five - Seven

2

1
Orange

3

Sew to Part One - Four

FACE ONE
PART TEN

1

Orange
2

Sew to Part Nine

Sew to Part Eleven

3

FACE ONE
PART THREE

1

Sew to Part Two

2
Orange

Sew to Part Four

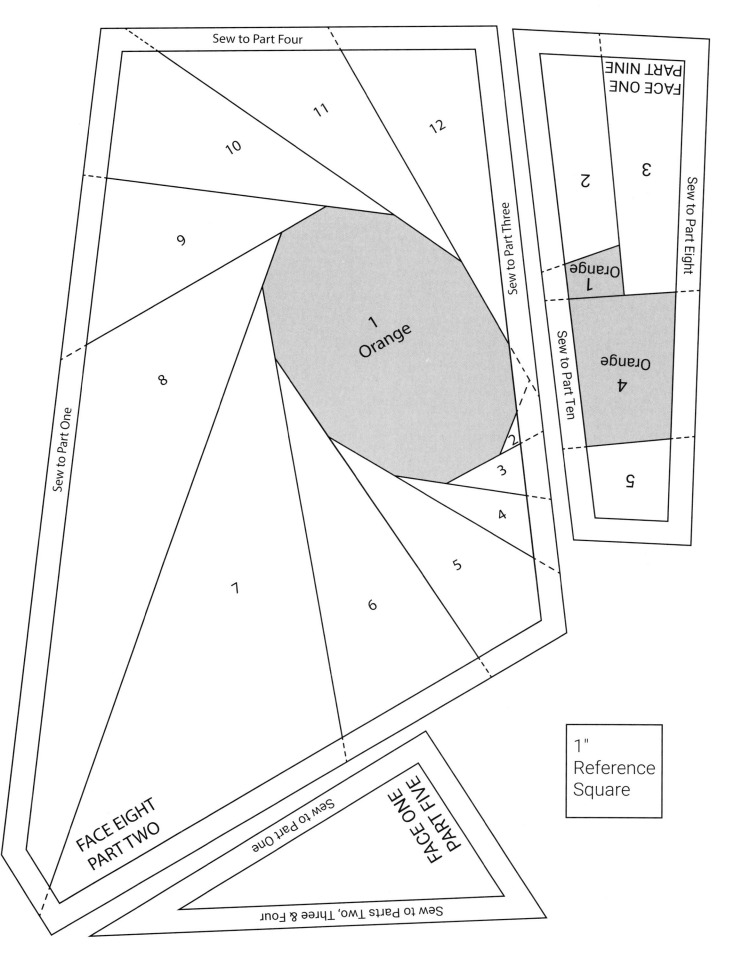

Sew to Part Four

11

10

12

Sew to Part Three

9

1
Orange

Sew to Part One

8

2

3

7

4

6

5

FACE EIGHT
PART TWO

Sew to Part One

FACE ONE
PART FIVE

Sew to Parts Two, Three & Four

FACE ONE
PART NINE

2

3

Sew to Part Eight

1
Orange

Sew to Part Ten

4
Orange

5

1"
Reference
Square

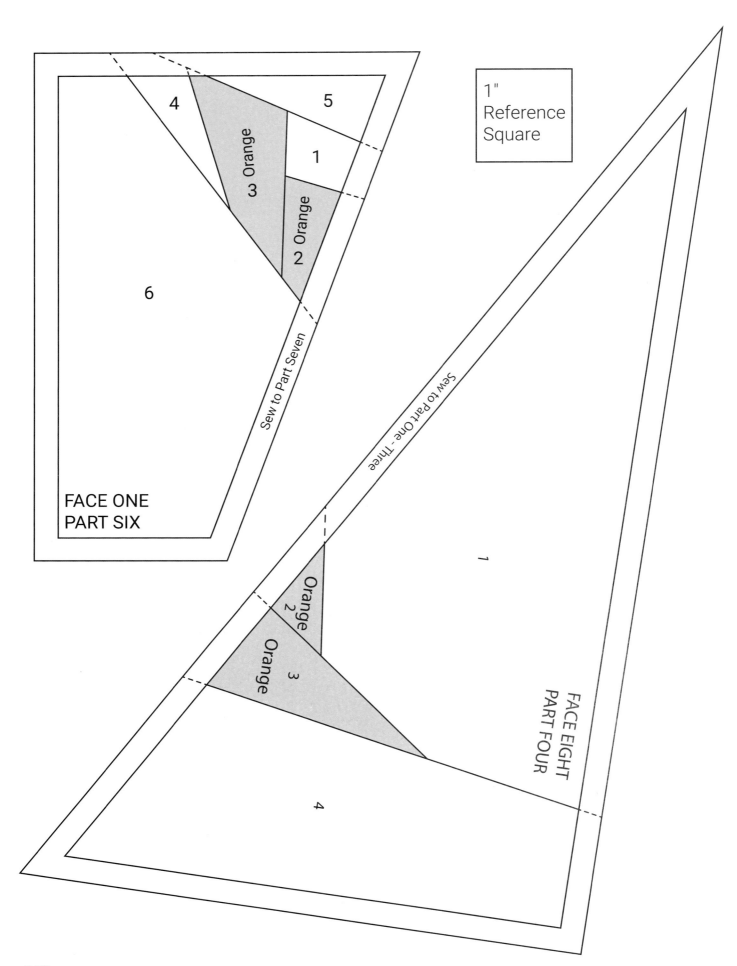

1"
Reference
Square

4

5

1

3 Orange

Orange 2

6

Sew to Part Seven

Sew to Part One - Three

FACE ONE
PART SIX

Orange 2

Orange 3

1

4

FACE EIGHT
PART FOUR

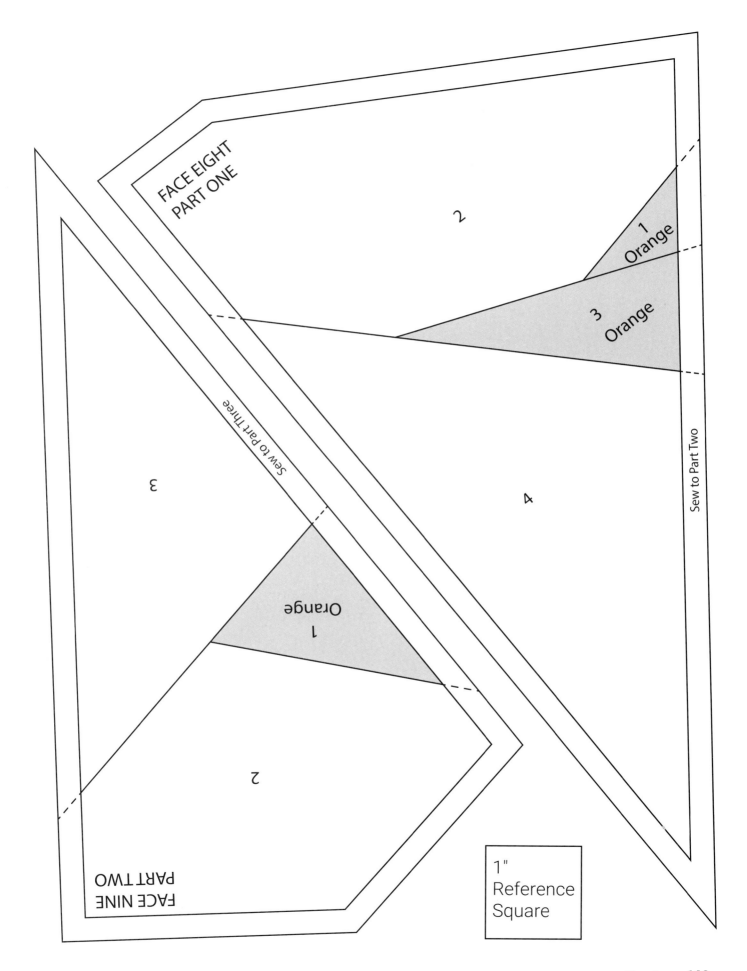

FACE EIGHT
PART ONE

2

1
Orange

3
Orange

Sew to Part Three

Sew to Part Two

3

4

1
Orange

2

FACE NINE
PART TWO

1"
Reference
Square

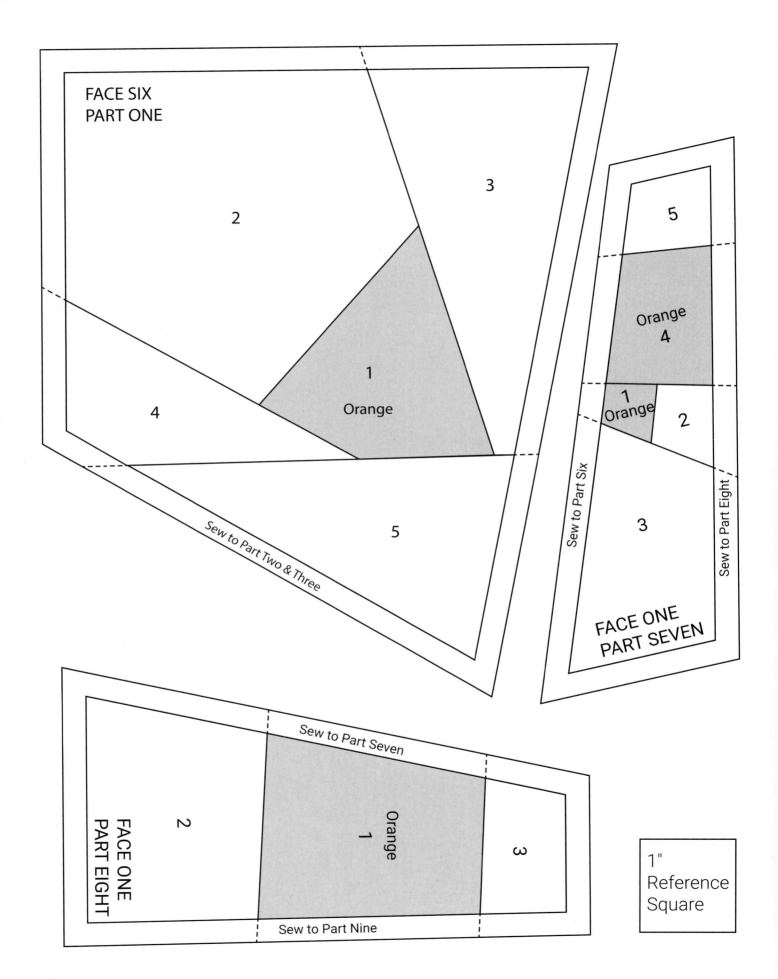

FACE SIX
PART ONE

2

3

4

1
Orange

5

Sew to Part Two & Three

5

Orange
4

1
Orange

2

Sew to Part Six

3

Sew to Part Eight

FACE ONE
PART SEVEN

FACE ONE
PART EIGHT

2

Sew to Part Seven

1
Orange

3

Sew to Part Nine

1"
Reference
Square

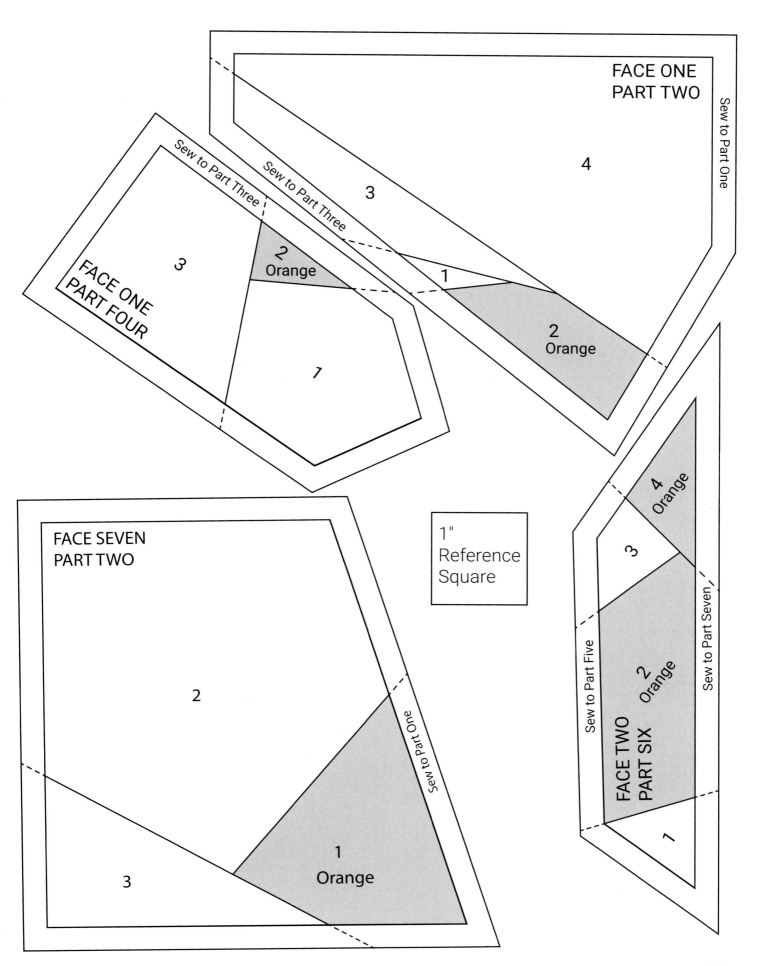

FACE ONE
PART TWO

Sew to Part One

4

3

Sew to Part Three

Sew to Part Three

3

2
Orange

1

2
Orange

FACE ONE
PART FOUR

3

2
Orange

1

4
Orange

3

Sew to Part Five

FACE TWO
PART SIX

2
Orange

Sew to Part Seven

1

1"
Reference
Square

FACE SEVEN
PART TWO

2

Sew to Part One

3

1
Orange

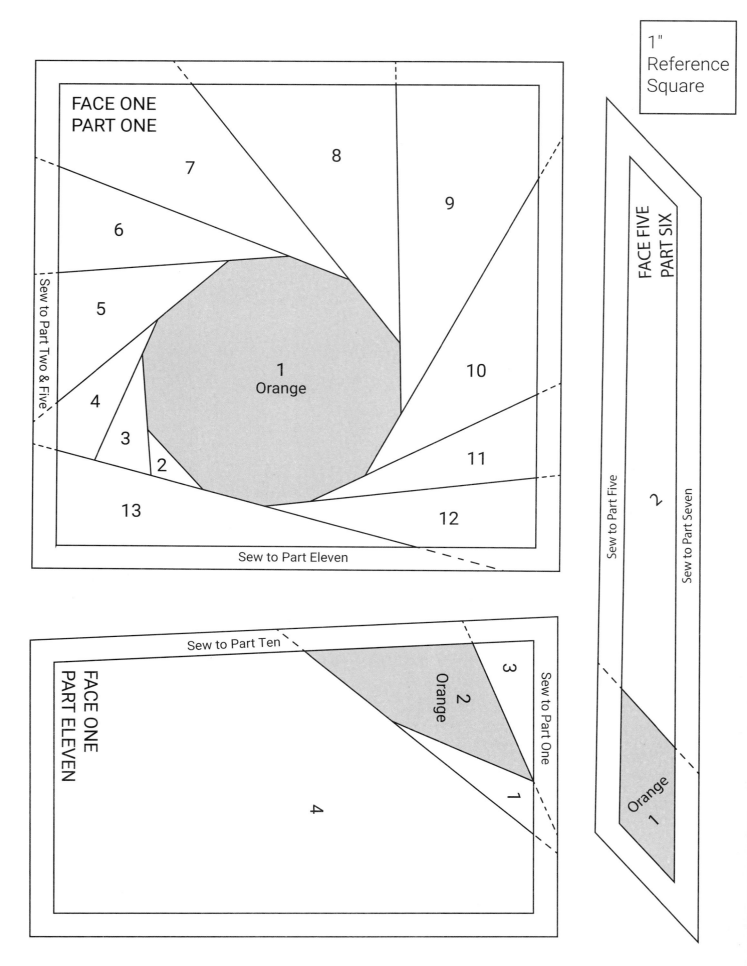

1"
Reference
Square

FACE ONE
PART ONE

7

8

9

6

5

Sew to Part Two & Five

4

3

2

1
Orange

10

11

13

12

Sew to Part Eleven

FACE FIVE
PART SIX

Sew to Part Five

2

Sew to Part Seven

Orange
1

Sew to Part Ten

3

2
Orange

Sew to Part One

1

FACE ONE
PART ELEVEN

4

Storage Bin Templates

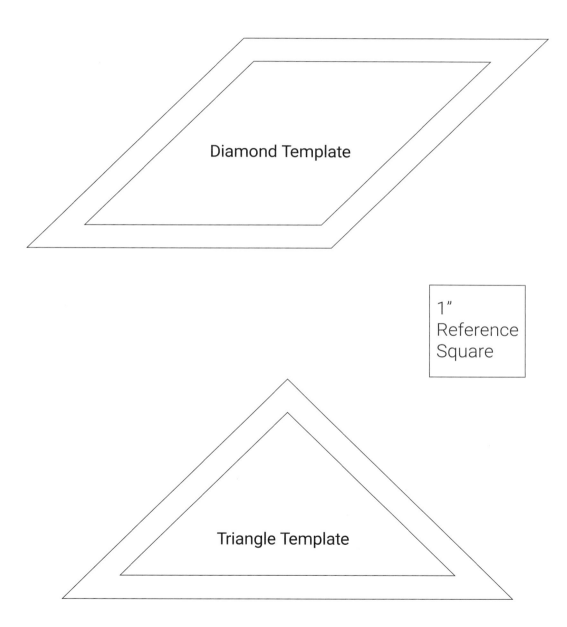

Diamond Template

1"
Reference
Square

Triangle Template

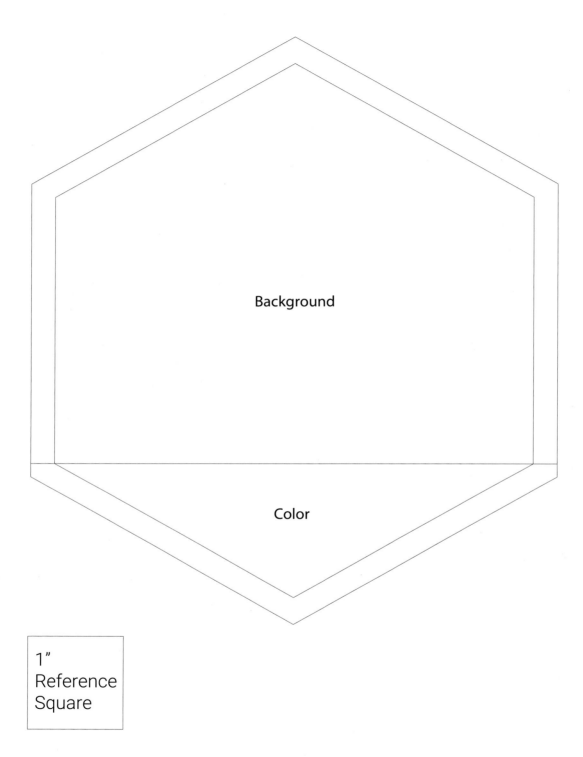

Background

Color

1"
Reference
Square

Mod Quilter's Baseball Cap Templates

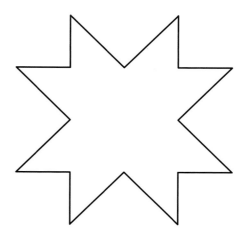

1"
Reference
Square

About the Author

I grew up in northern Virginia, just south of Washington DC. I went to college in Idaho and got my degree and my husband. Score! Eventually, we found ourselves nestled in the foothills of the Blue Ridge Mountains in West Virginia. Life moves a little slower here and we love it!

Both my husband and I currently work in fields that neither of us went to school for or got degrees in. My degree is in Medical Assisting. I worked one job in the field and decided it was not for me. As our family started to grow, I searched for ways to keep my mind and creativity busy while staying at home with our children. I sold for several direct-selling companies and had great experiences and made great friends. But a slow burn had begun, and it eventually turned into a bonfire.

As fate would have it, I married into a quilting family! With the help of my mother-in-law, I made a quilt for our first baby while I was pregnant. I fell in love with this new form of art. I loved working with the fabric and creating fabric puzzles that turned into keepsakes that my family enjoys every day.

In 2015, I turned my hobby into a business and began to long arm. It was a lot of work, but it was always humbling and exciting to be given someone's work of art and put my stamp on it. I absolutely loved working on my long arm and bringing quilts to life!

Over the years, my interest in quilting shifted to designing quilt patterns. Once I got the hang of that, I hit the ground running! I began publishing my own quilt pattern designs and eventually started a digital quilting magazine for the modern quilter, called *Modish Quilter Magazine*. The magazine has become my pride and joy, and I have loved teaching and bringing the modern-quilting community closer together.

It has been an amazing journey that I am so thankful for. And now I want to share what I have learned along the way to other quilters! I think it is important to learn and grow as a textile artist. This book is geared toward teaching new techniques and building skills so that you can feel unstoppable on your own artistic quilting journey.

For even more skill-building techniques, patterns, and a video-tutorial package, visit my website: www.kileysquiltroom.com

You can find more of my work at: www.modishquilter.com

Thank Yous and Credits

Thank you to my mother and mother-in-law who got me into crafting/sewing/quilting. Thank you to my father who instilled in me an entrepreneurial spirit. Most of all, thank you to my husband for believing in me and supporting me through all the ups and downs. You are my rock.

I could not have made this book come to life without the help of many other friends and supporters as listed below:

Megan Saenz of The Quiltographer:

• Made the Starry-Eyed Quilt

• Made the Countdown Chain links

• Photographed all photos

Maggie Blakley of Miss B's Quilting Studio:

• Made the Gaggle Pincushion and Thrashcan

• Made the Storage Bin Slipcovers

• Longarm quilted over half of the quilts

Hobbs Batting:

• Provided all the 100% premium cotton batting

Art Gallery Fabrics:

• Provided all the fabric for this book

I have been quilting for over 10 years and have used many fabrics from various manufacturers and shops. Hands down, Art Gallery Fabrics® are my favorites! I love how soft and silky they feel while not losing any of the quality of a good quilting cotton. My quilts always end up looking and feeling amazing! have also had an amazing experience and relationship with the AGF team and have so much respect for their company. AGF Pure Solids and prints are always going to be my recommendation to any quilter wondering what fabric to buy. You'll never go back!

Index

Note: Page numbers in *italics* indicate projects and templates (in parentheses).

Conversion Chart

inches	centimeters	inches	centimeters	inches	centimeters	yards	metric
⅛"	0.3cm	12½"	31.8cm	40½"	102.9cm	⅛ yard	11.4cm
¼"	0.6cm	13"	33cm	41"	104.1cm	¼ yard	22.9cm
½"	1.2cm	13½"	34.3cm	42"	106.7cm	⅓ yard	30.5cm
¾"	1.9cm	14"	35.6cm	42½"	108cm	½ yard	45.7cm
1"	2.5cm	14½"	36.8cm	44"	111.8cm	¾ yard	68.6cm
1½"	3.8cm	15"	38.1cm	45"	114.3cm	1 yard	91.4cm
1¾"	4.4cm	15½"	39.4cm	45½"	115.6cm	1¼ yards	1.1m
1⅞"	4.8cm	16"	40.6cm	47½"	120.7cm	1½ yards	1.4m
2"	5.1cm	16½"	42cm	48½"	123.2cm	1¾ yards	1.6m
2¼"	5.7cm	17½"	44.5cm	50"	127cm	2 yards	1.8m
2⅜"	6cm	18"	45.7cm	52"	132.1cm	2¼ yards	2.1m
2½"	6.4cm	18½"	47cm	52½"	133.4cm	2½ yards	2.3m
3"	7.6cm	20"	50.8cm	56"	142.2cm	2¾ yards	2.5m
3¼"	8.3cm	20½"	52cm	60"	152.4cm	3 yards	2.7m
3½"	8.9cm	21½"	54.6cm	60½"	153.7cm	3¼ yards	3m
3⅝"	9.2cm	22"	55.9cm	62½"	158.8cm	3½ yards	3.2m
4"	10.2cm	22½"	57.2cm	63"	160cm	3¾ yards	3.4m
4¼"	10.8cm	23½"	59.7cm	65"	165.1cm	4¼ yards	3.9m
4½"	11.4cm	24"	61cm	66"	167.6cm	4½ yards	4.1m
5"	12.7cm	24½"	62.2cm	66½"	168.9cm	4¾ yards	4.3m
5¼"	13.3cm	25½"	64.8cm	70"	177.8cm	5 yards	4.6m
5½"	14cm	27½"	69.9cm	72"	182.9cm	5¼ yards	4.8m
6"	15.2cm	28"	71.1cm	80"	203.2cm	5¾ yards	5.3m
6¼"	15.9cm	28½"	72.4cm	84"	213.4cm	6 yards	5.5m
6½"	16.5cm	30"	76.2cm	84½"	214.6cm	6¼ yards	5.7m
7"	17.8cm	30½"	77.5cm	87"	221cm	6½ yards	5.9m
7½"	19cm	31½"	80cm	87¼"	221.6cm	6¾ yards	6.2m
8"	20.3cm	32"	81.3cm	90"	228.6cm	7¾ yards	7.1m
8½"	21.6cm	33½"	85.1cm	90½"	229.9cm	8¼ yards	7.5m
9"	22.9cm	35½"	90.2cm	91"	231.1cm	8½ yards	7.8m
9½"	24.1cm	36"	91.4cm	96"	243.8cm	9 yards	8.2m
10"	25.4cm	36½"	92.7cm	96¼"	244.5cm	10 yards	9.1m
10½"	26.7cm	37"	94cm	98"	248.9cm		
10¾"	27.3cm	37½"	95.3cm	112"	284.5cm		
11"	28cm	38"	96.5cm				
12"	30.5cm	40"	101.6cm				